What to Expect When Your Wife Is Expanding

What to Expect When Your Wife Is Expanding

A Reassuring Month-by-Month Guide
for the Father-to-Be,
Whether He Wants Advice or Not

Thomas Hill, Registered Father

**Andrews McMeel
Publishing, LLC**

Kansas City

07 08 09 10 11 RR2 10 9 8 7 6 5 4 3 2 1

ISBN-13: 978-0-7407-6752-4
ISBN-10: 0-7407-6752-6

Library of Congress Control Number: 2007060673

www.andrewsmcmeel.com

ATTENTION: SCHOOLS AND BUSINESSES
Andrews McMeel books are available at quantity discounts with bulk purchase for educational, business, or sales promotional use. For information, please write to: Special Sales Department, Andrews McMeel Publishing, LLC, 4520 Main Street, Kansas City, Missouri 64111.

This one is for my second edition: Parker, Bixby, and Walker/Carter/Duncan (as of press time he hadn't arrived and we hadn't settled on a name yet—sorry, pal!)

Contents

Contents

What You May Be Concerned About
    Going Back to Work
    Safety Can Be Fun
    Flying Babies
    The Farmer in the Dell
    Superman Syndrome
    Postpartum Medical School Syndrome

Preface

How This Book Was Conceived ... Again

While writing the original edition of this book in 1992, I had a three-year-old and a one-year-old, and plenty of fresh, personal advice for prospective dads. Today, writing in 2007, I still have plenty of fresh personal advice because I find myself with a three-year-old and a one-year-old, with one more on the way. (And wonderful eighteen- and sixteen-year-olds, of course.)

I know, I know. Divorce, remarriage, five kids. It does seem like a lot of trouble to go through just to make sure that the revised and expanded edition you hold in your hands is a thoroughly accurate and up-to-date accounting of a father's experience at the dawn of the twenty-first century. That's just the kind of author I am. Dedicated. I've even managed to lift enough heavy babies to damage my wrist and thumb in a form of tendinitis that is called (I swear) "New Mom Syndrome." Apparently, it most often occurs in new mothers, whose ligaments have been loosened by pregnancy, then stressed by baby lifting. I don't know what excuse my ligaments can offer, but I can tell you I prefer the more scientific name—de Quervain's tenosynovitis—although I'd really prefer not to have it at all.

Now, cynics may question my judgment when it comes to writing about relationships. Let me assure you that, when it comes to relationships, I have never had the slightest idea what I'm talking about. I don't know what women want or why they do the things they do. Like most men, I simply remain dedicated to finding out, one baffling request at a time. And I can tell you that being happily married is much more fun than being unhappily married. So don't count on a third edition.

Enough about me. We are gratified the original edition met with such a positive reception. Over the years—even against many other competing titles—this slim volume has earned a loyal audience, apparently becoming a staple "new dad" gift along the way. We welcome this long-overdue opportunity to update and expand the book. There are numerous revisions throughout the entire book, alterations that reflect technological and medical advances, as well as a better representation of the cultural milieu of today's expectant dad. References to buying VHS tapes and the nymphet-like appeal of Madonna have been expunged.

What else has changed for expectant fathers in the past fifteen years? Plenty, from innovative health-care options to the burgeoning uses of the Internet, from the end of the cloth-versus-disposable diaper debate to the invention of the Diaper Genie (don't rub it three times . . . trust me). After all, back then ESPN was a young, underfunded cable network. Today, it's an irresistible juggernaut of sports entertainment—and at least a dozen children have been named "Espn" in its honor. Even minivans don't look quite as schoolmarmish as they once did—and if they really threaten your sense of manhood, you can fit plenty of car seats into an SUV. (Just don't go charging over dry creek beds while the kids in the backseat are trying to watch their DVDs of SpongeBob.) Today, everyone has a cell phone—so, theoretically, a golf outing for you while she is in her fortieth week is possible. That is just a theory, mind you; we don't know anyone who has tried it.

When it comes to pregnancy and childbirth over the last decade, there have been technical advances and further research, so that now there are literally scores of new fears, anxieties, and dietary restrictions to deal with. Luckily, provoking anxiety has gone totally out of fashion. Fifteen years ago, the core philosophy was that a new mother deserved to know every possible problem or outcome. Today, the experts agree that too much information breeds too much needless anxiety. So relax! When the time comes to worry about venous thrombosis or partial molar pregnancy, the doctors will tell you.

In all seriousness (for just about the last time in these pages), congratulations on your impending fatherhood, and best wishes to your wife as well. My only real advice is this: take care of each other, and the baby will take care of itself. Not *literally*, but, well, you get the point.

—Thomas Hill

Introduction

Why This Book Was Conceived

It used to be so easy. The rabbit would die; only her doctor had to hear the monthly details. After all, it was all in the realm of "female trouble." Dad's responsibility was to take one frantic drive to the hospital, spend a few hours pacing, and voilà! Progeny! Pass out the cigars. Those were the days when every newborn came with an undebated last name.

Everything has changed. Good news for those rabbits, but not for the expectant father. And in case you're wondering, yes, not so many years ago laboratory technicians really did have to knock off a bunny for every single pregnancy test that came out positive. But we are talking about today's father. He has a dozen new roles: birthing coach, dietician, masseur, interior decorator, butler, psychotherapist, and tugboat to the mother's barge. Furthermore, he is expected to be well versed in all of pregnancy's medical details, options, and research, up to and including the current issue of *The American Journal of Obstetrics and Gynecology*, and should be sensitive enough to know from across the room when the baby is kicking. All this, and he doesn't even get a healthy glow. What *about* the father?

What about *his* needs, *his* problems, *his* concerns?

We set out to write *What to Expect When Your Wife Is Expanding* for every man who is facing fatherhood. It is the book we wished we could have turned to in our own moments of crisis, self-doubt, and, perhaps most of all, boredom. Everything you need to know about the next nine months is in the pages that follow, although of course you don't really "need" to know anything, except possibly that *psychoprophylaxis* is the scientific term for birth preparedness training and does *not* mean birth control through telekinesis. And now you know that.

We have tried to be honest, factual, and reassuring. If, however, this book is generally terrifying, full of uneducated guesses, and peppered with reckless opinions, so be it. If we can make pregnancy easier for just one father, then it will all have been, well, actually, a complete waste of ink, paper, and man-hours. But if we can make pregnancy easier for five hundred thousand fathers or so, then it will all have been worthwhile.

Our critics—that is to say, our wives—may say that it is only fair that up until now all the books have focused on the female experience of pregnancy. Women are doing all the real work, right? Let's face it: you were only necessary for about fifteen minutes last July. No matter how much you do as a pregnant pop, nobody will ever practice kung fu on *your* bladder from the inside. Nobody takes over *your* body and soul for nine months. (Ten months actually; more on that later.) Isn't the woman doing all the real suffering? Isn't your wife the one who can't smoke one cigarette or have one glass of wine, and is supposed to drink milk by the pailful and can't eat any foods she likes and is gaining tons of weight anyway, which is completely unfair, and doesn't even know how she will deal with the pain and is doing it all because *you* were so gung ho on starting a family?

And why do you need your own book? Why can't you just read all her pregnancy books and empathize? First of all, women just don't understand how hard it is to empathize. Ironic, ain't it? Second, why should she begrudge you one measly, modestly priced book? Finally, her books are all really long and don't have very many jokes in them.

Yes. Yes. Yes. The pregnant woman is the one who really deserves all the attention. But you'll be hearing all that from her. You've got a pregnant mate, but now you've also got *What to Expect When Your Wife Is Expanding*. This is the other side of the story. We'll never call you a thoughtless slug. We know that facing all the new responsibilities, burdens, and duties of being a father, you need guidance, information, moral support. We know it's hard to be an expectant father, even when she doesn't. Remember, you're pregnant, too! (Just be very selective about how often you tell her that.)

A Note on Pronouns

It is traditional in books about pregnancy and child care for the authors to attempt to justify the use of the masculine pronoun when referring to a generic baby. Some rationalize that it's just less confusing when "she" refers to the mother and "he" refers to the baby (which leaves us fathers out entirely, as usual). Others find the compound "he or she" construction awkward. We are not so quick to bow to exigency and compromise.

Though it may take some getting used to, we have chosen to use an ampersand, slash, and dollar sign—&/$—to indicate the nominative "he or she" and a long row of eight asterisks—********—in place of the possessive "his or her." Our only concession to gender stereotyping is that in almost all cases we will assume the pregnant mother is a she.

But we have now changed our minds. (By the way, throughout the text I will be referring to myself as "we," just because it seems more authoritative.) The solution in the paragraph above is obviously unwieldy. Perhaps we could just assume that you're having twins, one boy and one girl? When your babies are born, they will be . . . no, that would be too anxiety provoking. Instead we will attempt to avoid the issue completely by writing around as many pronouns as possible. We will call a baby a baby, and will use the grammatically incorrect "their" when we really should say "his or her": for example, "When you first see your baby, you will want to nibble on their cute little toes." What do you want? Good grammar or gender neutrality? Furthermore, we may just slide into using "him or her" without even knowing it. Why are you reading this note anyway? Get to the text! You're having a baby, man, step to it!

Chapter One

What to Expect When ... "You're What?"

"You're What?"

Does life begin as "a gleam in Father's eye"?

This playful idiom is thoroughly outdated. Gleams are a nice start but, today, pregnancy is more likely to be planned, discussed, even scheduled. Couples consider their careers, their finances, their health, their age, the results of their genetic counseling, the feng shui of their apartment, and the latest forecast for mortgage rates. Having a baby is complicated, expensive, painful, and messy, yet people keep doing it. Scientists and sociologists point to an increasingly convincing body of research that indicates this is largely a result of babies being so darn cute.

So, a gleam in Father's eye? Quite the opposite, old boy. In fact, pregnancy may still begin with a gleam, but today that gleam is probably in Mother's eye, and she's not thinking about you, gorgeous. There comes a time in life when you're just the means to an eight-pound, two-ounce end.

There is, naturally, the possibility of simultaneous eye gleaming (and we all know how much fun that can be). This can mean either a pair of equally baby-crazy parents or a pair of very surprised ones who weren't expecting to be expecting. The former will probably invest in a wider variety of nursery wallpaper borders and baby books—but planners and nonplanners alike can be wonderful parents. Just because you're surprised doesn't mean you're not ready. Fate says you are, and the countdown to a new life—for you and the baby—started a month and a half ago.

Finally, there is the least common situation, when the gleam actually is in Father's eye. When *you* really want to have kids and your wife has lingering doubts about stalling her career, sacrificing her body, and learning to love the Wiggles and Dora the Explorer, well, that is *trouble*, mister. Danger, danger, danger! Sure, you might talk her into it but as the wait goes on, and the weight goes on—she'll know *exactly* whom to blame. If you're eager to get started having babies, be very careful to make it seem like it was at least partly her idea. You might even want to get her to sign something.

No matter whose fault, we mean, *idea* it is, so many joys and experiences lie ahead. Before you ever become a father, you're going to be "pregnant." You'll try to record the amplified heartbeat in the fourth month. You'll be parrying "Who's the father?" wisecracks from the boys. You'll nod knowingly, pretending you

3

see it, while a doctor points at a piece of abstract art and claims that is a sonogram image of Baby's head, spine, or "small parts." And then you'll have that ultrasound picture as a screen saver.

You'll go along with your wife when she puts your hand on her tummy and says, "There, you *had* to feel that one." You'll debate the issue of paternity leave. Can you take it? And if you take it, can you take it? How long can anyone take it? You'll organize the Date-Weight-Sex Trifecta betting pools at the office for fun and profit, and, if you're like the average man, you'll repaint the nursery 2.7 times before she likes the color.

You'll wonder about life with Baby. Will you ever see your single friends again? And how will you explain that yes, you do need to go home even though yes, your wife is capable of watching the baby alone? How can you man up, while wearing a baby in a sling? With a burp cloth draped over one shoulder? How will you deal with problems of rivalry? What will happen when you and the baby vie for your wife's attention? Have you properly bonded with your baby? Why do babies always pee the second the diaper is off? And how far does puke have to go to be defined as projectile vomiting?

But let's face it. If you've read this far, you're probably a pregnant dad, or possibly just a member of the author's family (hi, Mom! hi, Dad!), but, in ei-

ther case, you're committed. You're going to have to read the whole book. So go ahead. Take it one manly step at a time. This book will give you advice no other pregnancy book would give. That's a guarantee.

A Note to the Mother-to-Be

We couldn't be more pleased that you are being supportive of your husband and reading *What to Expect When Your Wife Is Expanding*. Or perhaps you're reading it because your husband was hiding it in his sock drawer. Perhaps you bought it for him—and want to make sure we're not out of line. Perhaps you've read every other pregnancy book you could find and are desperate. In any case, we're happy to have you here. Naturally, most of our comments are geared to a father's experience, but you shouldn't feel left out. Understanding what your husband is going through is the most important thing you can do. And don't forget: Pregnancy can be just as challenging, rewarding, and involving for a woman as it is for a man. Good luck!

By the way, perhaps we should be more open minded, and we have no intention of getting embroiled in any Red State/Blue State debate about family values, but we feel strongly that a man shouldn't get pregnant on his own. Call us old fashioned.

What It's Darn Important to Know About Prepregnancy Tests

Judging whether a woman is going to have a baby is a relatively simple matter of physiology. A home test or visit to a doctor can answer your question quickly and definitively. Judging whether a woman is in a state of prepregnancy is a much more difficult matter. However, it is vitally important for you to know if she is prepregnant. If such a condition exists, the sooner you know, the better. Once you know, you can institute either proactive or evasive action.

The simplest test for determining prepregnancy is to listen to your wife. She will undoubtedly express her desire for a baby, if not directly, then in suggestive comments: "Don't you think Zoë is a pretty name?" "Did you know there's a nice little nursery school just over on Elm Street?" or "My sister wants to know if we want Willy's crib now that he's out of it." These are clues. Are you picking up on them? If not, try reading this paragraph again. Think. What is this woman trying to tell you? Got it? There you go.

If listening to your wife is a challenge, if you had to read that last paragraph more than twice, or if you simply never know what she is getting at, it may be worth investing in one of the many books on the market aimed at improving male-female communication. A few recommended titles: Mary Cornwall, *What Women Don't Tell Men but Expect Them to Know* (Prentice-Schuster, 1999); E. P. Dunham, *Dictionary of the Female Language*, 15th edition (Oxford Reference Books, 2005); Robin Filmoore, *I Am Listening, You're Not Saying Anything!* (Freedentia College Press, 2003); D. Tanning, *You Just Don't Understand the First Thing About Women, You Ignorant Thick-Skulled Sexist Lout* (Scott-Foreswoman, 2004).

If you don't have time to read up on communication, or even to watch a little Dr. Phil, you still have the list below to help you make this important determination.

The early warning signs of prepregnancy:

POSSIBLE:

- Suggests having sex
- Switches to organic vegetables and buys a water filter for the sink
- Expresses new concern for your diet; buys you omega-3 supplements
- Buys a DVD of *Mary Poppins*—not to watch, just to have
- Suggests your study would make a nice bedroom
- Increases her use of cute nicknames: calls you "Li'l Bear," the cat "Meowzi," her toothbrush "the brusherwusher"
- Shows extreme, even giddy interest in other people's babies

- Displays renewed interest in real estate

PROBABLE:

- Changes the home page on your browser to babycenter.com
- Responds to your sexual advances by taking her temperature
- Continues to use cute pet names and now speaks in extended periods of baby talk: "Oh! 'itty Snuggums made all-gone with his beer"
- Keeps forgetting to use birth control
- Shows increased interest in the whole "stability" concept: pension plans, mortgages, dogs, neighborhood beautification projects
- Starts knitting baby booties, or knitting anything pastel
- Stops drinking
- Stops smoking
- Stops swearing, to set a good example

DEFINITE:

- Begins calling you "Daddy"
- Wants to make love twice a day for the three days around Thursday the twentieth
- Says, "I want to have a baby"
- Throws away her birth control
- Paints and furnishes a nursery
- Schedules a "conceptionmoon"—like a honeymoon, get it?
- Says, "I said, I want to have a baby."

What You Should Hve Known About Home Preganancy Tests *Before* You Bought This Book

Rapid Response, First Alert, EPT Warning System. Not only is it difficult to choose from among the many home pregnancy testing kits that are available, but all three of these are actually home smoke alarms—and you don't want to come home with the wrong thing entirely. If you do, of course you can cover by saying that your plans to start a family have made you more safety-conscious, but you still won't know if the bun is in the figurative oven. All you'll know is if there are buns burning in your literal oven. By the way, do not use the phrase "bun in the oven" at all until you have ascertained that your wife does not have a virulent reaction to it. Some women do.

The pharmaceutical companies have invested millions of dollars in the development of an accurate, dependable, and easy-to-use home pregnancy test. When these products first appeared on the market years ago, they were still untrustworthy, giving many false positives, false negatives, and occasional readings of "a negative times a negative is a positive," which is mathematically sound but leaves the pregnancy situation foggy. The early tests were approximately 75 percent as accurate as a good solid hunch.

Fabulous scientific breakthroughs, too complex for us to actually research, have since made these at-home tests remarkably accurate. Today, they are considered almost as reliable as a doctor's blood test, and who cares if your doctor is pregnant, anyway? Let her buy her own test.

Accuracy was achieved (at great expense, which you've probably noticed has been passed on to you, the consumer), but ease of use came more slowly. The early systems involved mixing chemicals, warming solutions, waiting for hours—and thus left much room for error. Worse yet, no one could decide on the appropriate indicator. Should a little strip turn pink? Should a little ball turn blue? Should a little cartoon stork appear? The choice of visual greatly depends on whether you are marketing these tests to hopeful young couples or to freaked-out high school seniors. For now, they seem to have settled on a relatively neutral design aesthetic: plus signs, or simple bars of color.

But look for niche marketing soon. The division is too vast to straddle. Perhaps the test will be named "Wild Thing" for the teen market, with the slogan "When ya gotta know right now, for sure." For the older crowd, something more high-toned, say, "Genesis," with the slogan "Be first to know." We certainly hope that both will still boast, as current products have, "Just hold it in your urine stream!" Now that's an appealing line of advertising copy.

The Job of Sex

Q. "We're not pregnant yet and, yes, we know how it's done, but ever since we started trying to get pregnant, sex just isn't what it used to be. And we're still not pregnant."

A. Science has shown compelling evidence that sex is linked to pregnancy. So don't give up on this basic approach. Until they start marketing in vitro fertilization kits over the counter, it appears that if you're going to have a baby, you pretty much have to do "it." This can be a complicated, tiring, and sometimes disorienting process, but don't forget that it can also be a loving and enjoyable one. Even fun, once you get the hang of it.

It may be hard to conceive but, for many couples, making the switch from recreational sex to procreational sex can be nerve-racking. Taking vitamin supplements, cutting down on caffeine and alcohol, checking the calendar, and taking the mom-to-be's temperature are not traditionally thought of as foreplay. Subconsciously, you may still have doubts about whether you are ready for fatherhood.

The exact reasons are unclear, but more and more research is pointing to stress as a cause of infertility issues. It makes sense. A woman already experiencing stress is probably not a good candidate for a cute little eight-pound stress maker. Some couples are now planning "conceptionmoons"—a vacation with the specific purpose of setting stress aside and letting nature take its course. Yes sir, nothing like a week away with no plans, no pressure, and no goal except to conceive a baby. That'll relax any guy.

Another factor on the plus side is that you are now working with the terrific advantage of not using birth control. (If you are still using birth control, that could be your problem right there.) In general, just try to forget about the ends and concentrate on the means. Think positive, and muddle your way through it—after all, once you have a baby, you'll hardly ever have sex at all!

Goo Goo Google

Q. "Do I really have to read a whole book about pregnancy? Before my brother-in-law gave me this book, I was just planning on doing a quick Web search whenever issues came up."

A. The Internet is a great place to get late-breaking injury reports on football players, watch YouTube videos of complete strangers embarrassing themselves in a stunning variety of ways, and try to re-acquire all the Dark Knight comics that your mother sold at a tag sale the week you went to college. However, it can be a dangerous place to get information about becoming a father.

Surfing the Internet is dangerous. It is not really like surfing at all, but more like being dragged (and clicked) out to sea by three different undertows. You will quickly find yourself swept away, floating untethered, drowning in a watery morass from which no amount of back-clicking can rescue you. Distractions lurk everywhere, from up-to-the-minute sports scores to wonderful opportunities in real estate to the latest news on Paris Hilton's "career."

Go ahead, Google "father" or "becoming a father," and before you know it you will be inundated with legal advice and firms offering to help you in your paternity battle to overcome the unfair prejudice toward mothers that is inherent in our judicial system. If you do need help in fighting for your paternal rights, Godspeed. But for the rest of us, it's just a lot of clutter. Imagine some medical question comes up. When you start searching, you'll find that, although all you want a few simple, reassuring answers, you'll actually have access to articles from medical research journals, complete with footnotes and laboratory methodology. Want information on babies? Whose? Angelina Jolie's? Celebrity baby photos are an Internet obsession that will do you little good. Want to see the incredible-but-true Web page about the world's first pregnant man? It's out there, drawing in the gullible with one of the most elaborate hoax sites ever created.

Now, there are indeed some worthwhile Internet resources. Babycenter.com is well decorated with sponsor links—but the core site has everything you need, including a way to register your due date and get weekly e-mails that will, at the very least, remind you to ask your wife how she is feeling. For those of you who just got married, making the switch from TheKnot.com to TheNest.com will be a comforting transition. For prospective fathers seeking a particularly macho approach—try Dad's Adventure, a vaguely military approach to diaper changing and baby wrangling.

All in all, let me assure you that your brother-in-law's purchase was a sound investment and well worth reading. This book is not only portable and easy on the eyes, but also tangible proof that you truly care about your wife's experience, the pregnancy, and every little symptom and possibility. That is gold, my friend.

Emotional Maturity

"Am I ready for this?"

Sure you are. Well, all right, maybe you're not, but your wife is and she can help you out with the fine points of emotional maturity. Anyway, by the time you're reading this book, the question is very likely moot. So why did you even ask?

If you are still having doubts, don't worry. Maturity isn't as complicated as psychotherapists would like you to believe. Becoming a mature, responsible, thoughtful, supportive, loving, giving, self-controlled, and self-aware person is really just a matter of behavior modification. Start with the list on the following page, find the immature behavior that you currently practice, and simply force yourself to choose the modified alternative. As you'll note, in some cases you don't even have to modify your behavior, just your explanation. After some initial backsliding, you'll find yourself behaving like a mature adult—as long as you stick to the chart. And in time, you may be acting like a grown-up simply out of habit. Before you know it, you'll feel ready to be a daddy. Then you'll have the baby, stop getting enough sleep, and completely regress, but you can cross that bridge when you come to it. In the meantime, get to work.

Immature Behavior vs. Modified Maturity

Immature Behavior	Modified Maturity
Openly and proudly collecting baseball cards	Scouting eBay to accurately assess the current market value of your collection
Buying new clothes to look good for chicks	Buying new clothes to look good for your superiors at work
Needing time alone to chill	Needing time alone to work things out
Buying a car that has great acceleration and sleek lines	Buying the same car because it has antilock brakes, extra room in the back, LATCH seat restraints, and a good write-up in *Consumer Reports*
Never making the bed because you're just going to get back into it again	Making the bed because it's a relatively easy way to make your wife happy
Drinking too much when out with friends	Drinking too much in the privacy of your own home
One-ringing your college roommate to let him know his team is getting thumped	One-ringing your college roommate to make sure your cell reception is working
Setting up a computer program to keep track of your fantasy football team	Setting up a computer program to keep track of your family finances
Playing the stereo too loudly	Telling the neighbors they're playing their stereo too loudly
Watching the game	Checking the score
Collecting beer cans	Recycling beer cans
Being proud of eccentric friends from college	Being concerned about eccentric friends from college

A Bundle of Joy

Q. *"How much does having a baby cost?"*

A. If you have to ask, you're grasping at straws. Cost is no reason not to have a baby. A baby can be absolutely free.

With home birth, breastfeeding, and gathering nuts and berries, by the time your child is six he will be pulling his own weight. However, the question remains: given a more typical contemporary lifestyle, can you afford a baby?

ITEM	COST	WHAT ELSE YOU COULD DO WITH THE MONEY	COST-SAVING TIP
Labor and delivery	$6,000–$8,000	Buy a decent used car	Consider home birth
Gifts, dining out, flowers to get wife through pregnancy	$3,200	Take an excellent domestic vacation	Compose poems and love letters instead
Pregnancy guidebooks, baby name books, Spock in hardcover	$125	Salute Sam Raimi by buying DVDs of all the *Evil Dead* movies and the first two *Spider-Man*s	Borrow from ex-pregnant friends
Clothing (per year)	$950	Buy complete collectible reprints of *Batman* daily comic strips from the 1940s. Hey, you spend your $950 the way you want; that's what I want.	Wear hand-me-downs

Allowance ages 0–8	$3,000	Spend a seriously wild weekend in Vegas	Practice tough love
Haircuts, ages 0–18	$2,100	A decent plasma flat-screen HDTV	Cut hair at home
Education, through grade 12	$40K–$200K*	Finance a low-budget independent film	Raise a "child actor" to recoup cost
College (four years)	$240K	3BR, 2BTH, cntrl a/c, new mechs, patio, grg	Make kids leave home at sixteen/ get scholarships

*This vast discrepancy based on the possibility of paying for private schools; the $40K assumes public schools and is just the cumulative costs of such items as (for example only, your actual costs may vary) smocks, backpacks, field trip fees, pens, crayons, notebooks, replacement notebooks because the ones you brought home are the wrong kind, foam-core backing for project displays, replacing the school's pet hermit crab that disappeared somewhere in the house over the Christmas break, protractors, gym locker padlocks, SAT coaching, debate team road trips, proms (limo optional), and contributions to the PTA fund-raiser, the ski trip fund-raiser, the Thanksgiving food drive, and the cost of buying the seventy-three candy bars that remained unsold with no time left in the lacrosse team fund-raiser. And you thought babies were cute.

Chapter Two

Throughout Your Pregnancy

The Eight Danger Signals

Most of the little complaints and problems of pregnancy do not require that you turn off the ball game; however, the husband should familiarize himself with the following list of eight dangerous conditions that must be addressed without delay, and without the distractions of play-by-play announcers in the background. If they are ignored, serious long-term damage to your relationship is a very real possibility.

Pay attention to your wife at once if you should notice any of the following conditions:

1. *Glamour-itis.* She is staring down at a magazine and flipping the pages very fast and hard, so that it appears that she isn't actually reading but is most interested in the noise she's making. And the impact it is having on you.

2. *Lactose Intolerance.* Not the traditional digestive form of lactose intolerance, but a more psychological version. To meet the high demands for calcium, drinking lots of milk is recommended. Many women try to make do with ice cream and little chocolate-flavored calcium chews. Others dutifully drink milk until they . . . well, lose it. Be prepared, she may serve you a pitcher of milk with your dinner, though you seldom drink the stuff. She may mention or imply that she is tired of drinking six to eight glasses of calcium-rich milk every day. She may also follow up with a few comments: "Something wrong with your milk, dear?" "Why aren't you drinking your milk, dear?" In severe cases, she may even pour milk into your beer.

3. *"Fine" Response Syndrome.* She responds to every question or suggestion with "fine," or "sure, fine," or even "fine, that's just fine with me."

4. *Ophthalmoduct Flow.* A clear, odorless fluid seems to be leaking from her eyes and is often accompanied by shortness of breath, sobs, and the phrase "you never understand."

5. *Maternal Reflexism.* She leaves for her mother's without telling you. Call and say you didn't mean it, and *don't* say you have no idea what you've done.

6. *Tourella's Syndrome.* Symptomatically related to Tourette's syndrome, Tourella's is a periodic neurological response that is rarely serious. The typical victim, someone who seldom or never swears (almost always a woman), gets

angry enough to attempt an obscenity. These fledgling efforts are ineffective, awkward, and embarrassing for both parties. For example, when trying to call her husband a shithead, the typical Tourella victim will instead call him a shitty shit.

7. *Ironic Lyricism.* Her conversational responses tend to be more flowery and poetic than necessary. If you mention you'd like to catch the fight on the tube, she says, "The manly art of pugilism, ah yes, noble fisticuffs. What was it about 'the sweet science,' my darling? Do tell."

8. *Labor and/or Childbirth.* If your wife is in labor or is actually having a baby (see chapter 11 for details), then you should stop ignoring her for a minute and help out. Definitely take the iPod out of your ears. Don't guess at what to do, and don't run and boil towels—just do whatever your wife wants.

The Monthly Prenatal Checkups in Review

Of course, your wife would love it if you could make it to every appointment, but after you've weighed yourself on the scales and read the magazines, and read through the brochures on collecting and storing umbilical cord blood, there really isn't that much to do for fun. Anyway,

the ob-gyn offices in the hospital are on the same floor as the infertility clinic, so while you may think that you're being perceived as a thoughtful, even doting husband, the other people in the waiting room may be assuming you're there to fill a test tube.

In any case, there are some can't-miss appointments and others that aren't worth the price of admission. Here are our capsule reviews:

THE FIRST VISIT: Dull, lots of background medical history, information, basic tests. There are two important reasons to be there: to impress the doctor, and to firmly establish in your wife's mind that you are fully committed to being involved . . . go.

THE SECOND MONTH: Lovebeat, it's a heartbeat! Now that's entertainment! It may take a few minutes of sliding the walkie-talkie around in the goop on your wife's belly, but when they find that mile-a-minute heartbeat—it's a beautiful thing. So don't miss this one . . . go.

THE THIRD MONTH: Getting a little repetitive already. Your wife complains of strange ailments and symptoms and weight gain. The doctor says it's normal; it's to be expected. Thank you, see you next month, good-bye. A definite . . . pass.

THE FOURTH MONTH: More of the same. Your wife keeps trying to come up with something novel to worry about, and the doctor keeps saying it's all perfectly normal, you can't take two aspirin, and don't call me in the morning. Unless you think you should be there to prevent your wife from making up symptoms wholesale (feet swelling like balloons, freckle-spread, speaking in tongues) in an effort to have something to worry about . . . pass.

THE FIFTH MONTH: Make sure that you don't miss an ultrasound if your wife is getting one, especially if you've decided to find out the baby's gender, but otherwise . . . pass.

THE SIXTH MONTH: Besides the always-dramatic weigh-in, there isn't much excitement in the middle months. Unless you feel the need to protect yourself from defamation of character during visits to the doctor in this period, you can just be attentive during the at-home recap, and you can safely . . . pass.

THE SEVENTH MONTH: Did you know that, on average, the Asiatic elephant's gestation period is over twenty months long? The opossum, on the other hand, is pregnant for about twelve days. Share these interesting facts with your wife, but as for the checkup . . . pass.

THE EIGHTH MONTH: Still not too much real news, but now is the time for all good men to come to the service of their wives. The final weeks will be a battle; the approaching due date a bright beacon of hope and fear. It's time to start paying attention, and, at the very least, you want to make sure that when you rush into the hospital on the big day, you recognize your obstetrician. Learn her name now . . . go.

THE NINTH MONTH: Now the checkups come weekly, but they're also packed with excitement. Is the head down? Can the doctor guess the weight? Does the due date seem right? Should we just head straight over to the hospital? How early should the baby be taught a second language? As frequently as you can . . . go.

THE SIX-WEEK POSTPARTUM: During labor and childbirth you, your wife, the obstetrician, and the nice nurse (not the sullen one) bonded into a devoted, affectionate team. Now it's time for a reunion, when you can show off the gem you all produced . . . go.

WHAT YOU MAY BE CONCERNED ABOUT

Q. Eating Right

"I've tried to be supportive, and have joined my wife in eating meals that are planned around her special dietary needs during pregnancy. But I'm concerned. Am I doing the right thing?"

A. Too many perfectly well-intentioned husbands fall into the same trap. What they fail to realize is that a father's special dietary needs are quite different from a pregnant mother's. Your metabolism is different; you are not carrying the child; your needs for iron and minerals are quite different. Simply put, you can eat anything you like. The big question is, will she let you?

For most expectant fathers, lunch becomes the key meal. After a modest bowl of iron-rich raisin bran for breakfast and with a low-carb spinach salad waiting for you at the end of the day, the midday meal is vital. You're at work, away from her watchful eye. It is often your only chance to depart from the dietary guidelines your pregnant wife is "sharing" with you. The following recommended foods will help you maintain your health throughout your wife's pregnancy. Remember, these are only recommendations—you should feel free to eat whatever you like, whenever you like, until you make yourself queasy.

THE RAW: Uncooked foods are risky to your wife for all sorts of hard-to-spell medical reasons, so you'll have to keep them to yourself. But that's no reason to miss out on the thrill of eating oddly textured food with the ever-present danger of food poisoning. Go for it!

Sushi

Steak tartare

Rare steak

Any meat bought from street
 vendors: hot dogs, red-hot
 sausages, souvlaki, shish kebab

JUNK: Empty calories are dangerous to the well-balanced high-protein, high-calcium diet. But whose diet is that? Not yours. Selections from the empty-calorie food group are the perfect accompaniment to a football game, working late, or just getting through the midafternoon doldrums.

Potato chips

Pressed potato product in
 chiplike form

Doughnuts

Popcorn (buttered, see below)

Candy

Cheese puffs

THE GREASY: Her intestinal balance is easily disturbed; yours can take it. Prove it to her by eating whatever you dang well please, and plenty of it.

Pizza

French fries

Corn dogs
Grilled cheese
Pastrami

THE SPICY: Especially during the period of morning sickness but also throughout pregnancy, heavily spiced foods are exclusively the male province.

Biriyani
Szechuan food
Slim Jims
Mexican food

THE STINKY: The mere smell of some foods can disturb the pregnant female, so eat 'em at the office and let your co-workers deal with it.

Thick soups: mulligatawny, minestrone, split pea
Stinky cheeses: Gorgonzola, Saga blue, etc.
Peanut butter
Wiener schnitzel and sauerkraut

Other Dietary Restrictions

MERCURY: Remember Mercury Morris? The Dolphins' running back under those great Don Shula teams? With Jim Kiick and Larry Csonka? Probably before your time, but think about it: have there ever been three more poetically named running backs in one era, much less on one team? Mercury, Kiick, Csonka. If Charles Dickens had written *Semi-Tough* . . . but we digress.

Fish apparently have too much mercury in them.

ALCOHOL: While discouraged for the mom-to-be, beer is an essential part of any future father's daily intake. It has vitamins B_6 and B_{12}, nutrients that are vital to your immunological system or bone formation or something like that. In any case, we recommend a good cheap local beer. Fresh and served uncomfortably cold. Two or three taken internally each evening will provide a salubrious spiritual cushion.

CAFFEINE: Not recommended for pregnant women, but for you? What better way to jump-start your day? And your body needs caffeine, especially during times of stress and exhaustion. It would be best if you drank a whole lot of coffee, pretty much all day long, along with the occasional Red Bull, but caffeine can also be found in smaller amounts in tea, in some sodas (which also supply large amounts of vital sugar), and in chocolate. If it interferes with your ability to sleep . . . well, just you wait.

Breakdown of Your Wife's Weight Gain		Breakdown of Your Wife's 7-Lb. Maternal Fat	
Baby, etc. (placenta, amniotic fluid, uterine enlargement)	12.75 lbs.	Milk fats	2.75 lbs.
		Eating for two	1.5 lbs.
Maternal breast tissue	1 lb.	Tasti D-Lite or your local equivalent: TCBY, et al.	.75 lb.
Maternal blood volume, fluids in maternal tissue	5.75 lbs.	Office birthday cakes it would have been impolite to refuse	.5 lb.
Maternal fat (see adjoining column for complete details)	7 lbs.	Just-one-bites from husband's desserts	2.5 lbs.
Total Average Gain	**26.5 lbs.**	Unfair, inexplicable, punishment-from-God weight gain	1.75 lbs.
		Ben & Jerry's	1.5 lbs.
		High-salt, high-fat, bagged junk foods too embarrassing to mention by name	1.75 lbs.
		Total 7-lb. Gain*	**13.5 lbs.**

*The difference between the 7-pound average gain and the 13.5 pounds of maternal fat we calculated cannot be explained. It just kinda snuck up on us.

When Not to Call the Practitioner

You should, of course, familiarize yourself with the symptoms and problems that you should immediately report to your doctor—severe abdominal pain, spotting or bleeding, severe headache, visual disturbances, fainting, dizziness, chills, or fever. However, it is also important to know what symptoms do *not* require immediate attention. By studying these symptoms you can save yourself pointless and time-consuming jaunts to the local hospital.

- Sudden or severe crankiness
- Gradual enlarging of the belly area
- Everything going too smoothly
- A sudden increase in thirst, swelling or puffiness in the hands, severe headaches, fever, fainting, dizziness, sudden weight gain, nausea, or visual disturbances when they occur in the father
- Crying during sappy made-for-TV movies, when sad songs are played on the radio, or when there are really cute kids on commercials
- General worry
- Need for makeup tips to accentuate "healthy glow"
- Sudden worry about the state of public schools in your area
- Tivo keeps choosing to record shows you have no interest in

- Your inability to feel the fetal movement even though your wife insists you ought to be able to
- Occurrences of any unusual symptoms listed in pregnancy guidebooks, in your sister's friend who is pregnant
- Doctor gave an odd-numbered due date, and your wife's always hated odd numbers
- Constant clumsiness and spilling of drinks
- Inability to decide on a name, especially during the first trimester
- Your wife's foot has gone to sleep
- Inability to find anything good to watch on TV

Exercise

"We've gotten all sorts of information about exercise for my wife: the Kegel, dromedary droops, and pelvic tilt exercises. What is the right form of exercise for a pregnant father?"

A good rule of thumb is that the easiest exercise is no exercise at all. Occasionally thinking to yourself that you ought to get started on some program but then thinking you don't look *that* bad and realizing that a pretty good hockey game is on TV may not do you any good, but it sure is relaxing.

Still, if you do want to get in shape to help your wife through her pregnancy and to prepare yourself for the rigors of early fatherhood, there are some specific exercises that can help. Remember, you're pregnant, too! So start slowly, don't strain, taper off during the last trimester, and avoid contact sports like football, rugby, and extreme cage fighting.

WIFE CATCHING: Stand in a relaxed position, feet spread slightly, knees bent. Then have an assistant tip a double mattress in your direction. Catch the mattress, then lead it out of the room without breaking any furniture. Repeat, and when you reach a high success level, you'll be well prepared to help your wife maneuver in crowded restaurants in her ninth month.

LABOR COACH'S NECK TILT: To prepare yourself for a long and sleepless labor: Sit in a comfortable position. Allow your eyelids to fall slowly over your eyes and tilt your neck to one side; then suddenly jerk your head straight up, open your eyes, and say, "Yes, honey?" Repeat fifteen or twenty times daily.

BASIC KEGEL EXERCISES: Join your wife when she does her Kegels. Lie on your back, with your head supported and your knees up. Let your arms lie flat at your sides. Slowly tense and then relax the muscles in your penis. Do at least twenty-five repetitions. It may not have any particular benefit, but it's a hell of a lot more pleasant than most exercises. And no, you don't have to stretch out first.

STROLL-UPS: Hold a twenty-pound weight under one arm. Stoop down, bending at the knees unless you don't want to, and, using your one free hand, change the battery in your watch, stand, and repeat. (This exercise will prepare you for the process of opening or closing a portable stroller while holding baby in one arm.)

RUNNING: Sit up suddenly from a comfortable seat. Raise your left arm, pulling your hand outward to reveal your watch. Tilt your head toward your left wrist and say, "Oh shoot, I've gotta run." Get up and leave, making sure your right hand has opened completely and left the beer on the bar.

What Not to Do

"She's pregnant, but she won't lie down. My wife is still working, jogging, everything. Isn't a pregnant woman not supposed to lift anything, or do anything?"

Unless her doctor advises otherwise, pregnancy should not prevent your wife from engaging in any of her ordinary activities. Work, sex, even noncontact sports are all okay. There are, nonetheless, some restrictions. The following activities are to be avoided—as much as possible—as soon as she knows she is pregnant

Limbo dancing

Bungee cord jumping

Tournament Twister

Rewiring your home using do-it-
yourself handbook

Slam dancing

Playing box lacrosse

Asbestos removal

Driving in demolition derbies

Touring sites of nuclear accidents

Sword swallowing

Riding the NASA centrifuge to
test g-force endurance

Bear-baiting

Freedom fighting as a mercenary
in Central America

Time travel

Quitting Smoking Now

"I'm trying to quit smoking so my wife and the baby won't have to deal with my secondhand smoke, but I just can't seem to break the habit."

Listen up. You're eating what you want. You're still knocking off a few brews each evening and keeping your local Starbucks in business. Shouldn't you give up something in the spirit of solidarity? Sure, your father didn't have to quit smoking, but that was then, this is now. It is the least you can do, and living longer isn't a bad side benefit. Watching your kids grow up will give anyone a refreshed desire to stick around for as long as possible, just to see how it all comes out.

Now, outwrestling the nicotine monkey is never easy, and with the oncoming responsibilities of family—the accelerating financial demands, the endless emotional stress, the constant demands on your time—well, frankly, you deserve to sit back and enjoy some real tobacco satisfaction. Don't do it! Put it out right now. You *can* quit—you can handle it all, and without your thin white pals.

The key to quitting is to determine which aspect of smoking appeals to you the most. Is it the nicotine? Or is it oral gratification? Or just something to do with your hands? Think about it. What do you miss the most? After you decide why smoking appeals to you, just look on the following chart for a simple, healthful substitute. After you use the substitute to wean yourself from the noxious weed, then you can work on kicking the substitutes. If you can't, just remember: Scientists have proven that cigarettes are *not* dangerous to your health. (Until you light them on fire and suck on them.)

Appealing Aspects of Smoking	Substitute
Effects of nicotine	Try the patch, chewing tobacco, snorting snuff
Something to do with your hands	Eat Pixy Stix candy all day long; learn card tricks; grow facial hair and smooth it a lot; scratch privates frequently
Morning headaches	Drink too much, especially warm gin and/or tequila
Just enjoy dependency	Take up another addiction: caffeine, gambling, watching television
Carbon monoxide	Inhale automobile fumes, either by taking walks near heavy traffic or in the privacy of your own garage
Yellow staining of hands and mustache	Use food coloring
Dizziness and nausea	Spin in fast circles
Enjoy handing money to local merchants for something that does you no good whatsoever	Buy lottery tickets
Smelling bad	Minimize tooth-brushing
Makes you look cool	Grow sideburns a little longer; get some serious tattoo work; never wear sweaters; get an eye patch

Chapter Three

The First Month

What Your Wife Will Be Complaining About

BEFORE SHE KNOWS:

🐣 Exhaustion

🐣 You

🐣 Not being pregnant after all these months of trying

🐣 Her college roommate who gets pregnant every time her husband looks at her

🐣 The cost of home pregnancy testing kits

🐣 That everyone else in the world seems to be pregnant; "what if we can't get pregnant?"

🐣 That you don't believe her when she says she "just feels pregnant"

🐣 Her voracious sexual appetite, or . . .

AFTER SHE KNOWS:

🐣 Her complete disinterest in sex

🐣 Why last month, or even the month before, would have been a better time to get pregnant, because it's miserable being pregnant in the winter (or summer, spring, or fall, as the case may be) and this bad timing is somehow all your responsibility

🐣 Heartburn and indigestion, flatulence and bloating

🐣 Heartburn and indigestion, flatulence and bloating in you, and what's your excuse?

🐣 That the hospital won't let you sign up for their childbirth preparedness classes until you're seven months pregnant

🐣 Aversions to certain foods— especially chicken soup right after you make a huge vatful

🐣 That romantic trip to Venice must happen now—when she feels horrible—or be delayed for a decade or so

🐣 Stretch marks (not actual stretch marks, just the concept of stretch marks)

🐣 Emotional highs and lows, fear, ecstasy, anxiety, and elation, often all at the same time

A Couple of Things to Say to Let Her Know You're Caring, Sensitive, and Up on the Required Reading

What your wife is expecting you to read is a whole stack of books, not including this one. To save you the trouble, we have read (all right, skimmed) dozens of books about childbirth and pregnancy, and gleaned a few interesting and relevant facts for you to memorize and use. Don't worry about getting caught; if she presses you for details, it's a simple matter to say, "Gee, I can't remember exactly where I read that—I've been through so many books now."

Unlike many other sections of this volume, the "Couple of Things to Say . . ." are based on actual, if limited, research, so you can actually *learn* while simply trying to make a good impression.

1. "One early symptom of pregnancy is that Montgomery's tubercles, sebaceous glands in the areola of the nipple, become prominent. Shall I check for them?"

2. "Among the battery of tests at your first visit to the ob-gyn will be the rubella titer that tests for immunity to German measles, so it doesn't matter that you lost your record of childhood immunizations."

3. "Margaret Mead's research in New Guinea found that in some societies, boils are considered a typical symptom of pregnancy."

What to Buy This Month

Your little bundle of joy will cost you a bundle well before you even get to take it home from the hospital. To help you organize and realistically assess your financial needs in the coming months, we have broken down all the necessary purchases into a set of monthly lists.

If you are superstitious, or just uncomfortable about buying things for the baby before the actual birth, then don't make these recommended purchases. There is no reason you can't buy everything you need after the baby has arrived safely (although the credit card company may get panicky and start asking stores to verify your identity).

ESTIMATED COSTS, MONTH ONE
Basics: $78
Basics plus extras: $200,078

What Your Wife May Look Like

Throughout the first month her eyes will be agleam, because intuitively she already knows. Her cheeks may be flushed, as she probably has a pretty good idea which night it was, too. She chooses the clothes she knows you like. Healthy glow? Yes, but alternating with the unhealthy greenish glow of morning sickness.

Basics

Home pregnancy test kit
The real *What to Expect When You're Expecting*
Dr. Spock
A baby name book
Vitamins—for you

Extras

A home in the suburbs
Anything listed in the "What to Buy" section of later months, because you can't wait until you actually know that you're pregnant
All the selfish luxury items you won't dare buy once you're a family man—box sets of CDs, single malt scotch, nice ties, season tickets, monogrammed poker chips

WHAT YOU MAY BE CONCERNED ABOUT

Sex During Pregnancy

"Okay, we're not even sure she's pregnant yet, but I'm worried already, so what about sex during pregnancy?"

The approach of fatherhood is a time full of tension, anxiety, and self-doubt. Sex can be the perfect way to relax and escape the pressures. Furthermore, there is no medical or physiological reason to prevent you from engaging in a full sexual life. However, like many men, you may feel uncomfortable about cheating on your wife, so sex is out.

Now might be a good time to take up a diverting hobby, such as collecting stamps, building plastic models, or watching too much TV. Keep yourself busy and you'll forget all about those troublesome urges, just like the old Boy Scout manual said.

Tippling for Two

"My wife had a few drinks before we knew she was pregnant. Could this be a big problem?"

Probably not. A better indicator of a problem is when the father has a *lot* of drinks *after* he finds out they're pregnant. That's a big problem. As for the young mother, certainly drinking during pregnancy is not recommended, but a few drinks are still statistically very unlikely to cause a problem for the baby. Stop worrying. A generation ago, midafternoon martinis were standard fare to help pregnant moms relax and unwind. Remember, in France, even very young children drink large quantities of wine with every meal, and look at France.

On second thought, maybe cutting back a little wouldn't hurt.

Gender Preference

"I foolishly expressed a slight preference for a boy. Now how do I convince my wife that I won't hate a girl?"

All is not lost. There are two tactics that might work:

The first plan is to say, "I only said that because I thought you had a slight preference for a boy; I would actually much prefer a girl." This lie must then be followed by a full-fledged propaganda campaign: buy pink booties, talk only about girls' names you like, call the baby "she" at all times, and mention that you heard that girls are much easier to toilet-train, which is true, by the way.

The other plan is to claim that you didn't say it at all; that in fact the cat said it. Be sincerely amazed that the cat talked. Wonder if there's someone you should call. The newspapers? The humane society? The president? Don't budge an inch, and eventually your wife may think that you are actually mentally disturbed and under too much pressure. Though not a long-term solution, it may give you enough time for things to cool down.

Judging by these solutions, of course, the best thing is to avoid the situation at all cost. Get your answer down pat now: You want a healthy, happy baby—whether it is a boy or girl is the furthest thing from your mind. Maintain this attitude without wavering, and you'll be all right. And don't feel bad. Let's face it, all men really have a slight preference for a boy, and all women really have a slight preference for a girl. It's a matter of sociobiology. First of all, we're all egoists, so replicating ourselves is job one. Men also want someone to toss a baseball with, not someone to play volleyball with; but, more than anything, it all comes back to your basic inability to understand women. No matter how cute a daughter is, you know that someday she will baffle you with her feminine mystique. Hoping for a boy is just as normal as hoping for a baby that speaks English. You want to understand what your child is saying, right?

Toxoplasmosis

"I've heard that I may be able . . . we may have to get rid of our cats because of the danger of toxoplasmosis."

If you've been dying for an opportunity to get rid of the mangy, soulless felines, read your wife the paragraph below; if you actually like cats, skip to the third paragraph.

Cat feces and raw meat often carry the parasitic organism known as *Toxoplasma gondii*. It causes a disease that—

although very mild; often it goes unnoticed in those who have its low-grade fever, swollen glands, and rash—poses a serious threat to the fetus of a pregnant woman. It can cause permanent damage, illness, or even death. Cats should be tested but in most cases simply sent away. You should also avoid contact with other people's cats, and avoid gardening in soil that cats may have used as a litter box.

The odds are high that if you have cats or eat raw meat regularly,* you long ago contracted the disease and are now immune. A simple, but not-covered-by-your-annoying-HMO test at the doctor's office can establish this for certain. Of the very small number of women who contract the disease, 60 percent don't pass it on to their fetus, and two-thirds of affected babies show no ill effects anyway. Also, damage is unlikely to occur in the first trimester. Just have your cat tested for an active infection, then keep it indoors, away from mice, birds, or other cats. And when pregnant, a woman should let her husband deal with the litter box.

You can dump the cats or keep them. In either case, you should avoid eating any raw or very rare meat. And it almost goes without saying that you certainly shouldn't eat raw cat.

*Who the heck eats raw meat regularly?

Chapter Four

The Second Month

What Your Wife Will
Be Complaining About

☘ Exhaustion

☘ You

☘ Morning sickness

☘ Midmorning sickness

☘ Afternoon sickness

☘ Dusk sickness

☘ Late-evening sickness

☘ Whoever named it morning sickness

☘ The "reassuring" pregnancy books, which terrify her because she can't stop rereading the "What could go wrong" sections

☘ Iron supplements and the inevitable constipation they cause

☘ That she wants to ask the doctor about the frightening condition preeclampsia but doesn't know how to pronounce it

☘ Sudden realization that child could inherit *your* nose

☘ How she's dying to tell everyone she's pregnant

☘ Her mother, who has happily informed you that she hasn't thrown out any of her three-decade-old baby clothes, and that the trunk is in the mail

☘ Fear that cats will be jealous

☘ Emotional highs and lows, fear, ecstasy, anxiety, and elation, often all at the same time

A Couple of Things to Say to Let Her Know You're Caring, Sensitive, and Up on the Required Reading

1. "That morning sickness is rough, honey, but at least you don't have hyperemesis gravidarum, the rare condition of severe and unremitting vomiting that must be treated with antiemetic drugs. Right?"

2. "Nitrates and nitrites in food can become potentially harmful nitrosamines, so we'll avoid eating cured or commercially prepared hams, bacon, sausage, luncheon meats, smoked fish, Chinese salt-dried fish, raw and smoked salmon or shad."

What to Buy This Month

It's never too soon to begin indulging in frivolities and all the things you remember from wherever you last saw actual babies. If it looks useful, buy it. If it looks cute, buy it. You, my friend, are a dad-to-be. You need these things.

ESTIMATED COSTS, MONTH TWO
Basics: $200
Basics plus extras: $350

Basics
Booties
Bicycle baby seat
Bicycling helmet
Busy box, to hang in crib
Crib mobile
Electric bowl (keeps gruel warm)
Jolly Jumper (actually these are hard to find, since they are obviously so unsafe—try eBay)
Onesies: the adorable little one-piece underwear with the snaps in the crotch
Port-a-Play: toys that you suspend over infants for batting practice
Silver spoon
Teething rings
DVD of *Dumbo*

Extras
Baby Shaders, to attach to the inside of car windows to protect the baby's eyes from the sun
Eton suit or tiny white lace gown, depending on what you're expecting
High-contrast black-and-white crib mobile
Mountain stroller: four-by-four stroller with high underbody clearance and independent four-wheel suspension
Euro-stroller: every few years, there is some new, funky stroller from Finland or Belgium or Sweden that looks like nothing you've ever seen and costs more than you ever imagined.

What Your Wife May Look Like

Toward the end of the second month she will wear, for the last time ever, that great pair of jeans she's had since college. She may think she's showing, since her belly isn't completely flat. Don't argue the point. Healthy glow? None. Complete takeover by the unhealthy greenish glow of morning sickness.

Or What a Friend of Yours May Be Concerned About

Q. "This friend of mine, not me, was wondering if there's any way of knowing if the baby is definitely his. More specifically, is there a way of establishing this without letting his wife know there is any doubt, because, as you can imagine, such a doubt could be extremely destructive to a relationship in and of itself, if you know what I mean."

A. Whew. You're in big trouble. If you can't find out, you'll be racked with doubts and anxieties. If you try to find out—well, right or wrong, if she finds out that you were trying to find out, it's over. One thing for sure: if you're not sure, and you're suddenly invited to appear on a daytime talk show . . . don't go!

We guess you just have to hope that your suspicions are not correct. Sorry, that's the best we are going to offer. It's certainly possible that there is a blood test or some other kind of test that could be done in conjunction with amniocentesis, but even in the name of research we wouldn't dare start asking questions about it. Get serious. A guy goes around asking those questions, claiming it's research, and before you know it, someone overhears, passes it on, and boom, marriage over. In this territory, even hypothetical questions are just too dangerous. Sorry. In fact I wouldn't even linger on this page too long if I were you.

The Interim Name

"We're pregnant, this is fabulous. There's nothing my wife and I would rather do than sit around talking about, well, him or her or it. What should we call our fetus? 'It' seems so impersonal."

Within your wife a new life has sprung into potentiality, and for the next nine months you will be obsessed with charting the development of the fetus into a baby, planning and sacrificing as you enter a new life as parents of . . . him, her, or it.

For some, the answer is simply to rely on women's intuition. Whatever your wife's hunch is—boy or girl—just assume she's right. (In case you haven't already picked up on this theme: assuming your wife is right is the central tenet of this pregnancy survival guide.) If she doesn't have a guess, don't worry—complete strangers will soon begin taking one look at your wife and telling you, "It's a girl because she's carrying low and wide," or "It's a boy because her skin looks so great." So just find a consensus and go with that gender.

If you're afraid of guessing wrong, creating false expectations, or possibly offending your unborn child, you might want to give it a nickname. It seems that every couple has their own unique moniker. One couple we know went with Herbie for reasons known only to themselves. Another called their baby-to-be "the Peanut," based on a pregnancy book's description of the two-month-old fetus. Still another well-organized couple picked a male and a female name, and spoke of "her/him" and "Megan/Daniel." (Actually, she/he was Megan/Daniel until the fourth month, when the husband had second thoughts and started calling her/him Megan/Charles, while his wife stuck with Megan/Daniel, and then after amnio results determined that they were carrying a boy, they settled on Michael, but that's probably a whole lot more complicated than you wanted to know. Although perhaps you should also know that when he was born, Michael became Jonathan and still is.)

So feel free to call baby-to-be whatever you like, whatever makes you comfortable, with the possible exception of cute diminutives of the scientific names. If you do fall into calling your baby-to-be Fetey, or Embry, keep it to yourselves.

Avoiding Couvade Syndrome

"I'm terrified that I may contract this couvade syndrome thing and get morning sickness, retain water, and have nightmares about stretch marks. How can I avoid a sympathetic pregnancy?"

Couvade syndrome is a psychosomatic condition also known as sympathetic pregnancy. Its male victim suffers from all the symptoms of pregnancy. In the most serious cases, his belly will actually swell. In less serious cases, he will simply suffer from morning sickness and general crankiness.

Common sense tells us that the best way to avoid a sympathetic pregnancy is not to be too sympathetic. For most men, this comes naturally, but many may need to work on it. At the first signs of morning sickness in yourself, don't panic but do take positive steps. Explain to your wife what's going on. When she understands that couvade syndrome is a legitimate medical condition, she will laugh with spiteful delight, but later on she will more than likely understand that right now you just need a little time to be cold, distant, and detached. If you can't absent yourself completely, try to ease off gradually from being sympathetic. Stop listening attentively to her complaints; promise to do little errands and forget them; and when she reads sections of pregnancy books to you, comment on the prose style or question her pronunciation of a word.

If your symptoms persist, you may even need to play little pranks on her: tamper with the bathroom scale, set all the clocks in the house back two hours, or replace her shoes with a pair a whole size smaller. There's no end to the fun you can have, and afterward you'll both share a good laugh.

Couvade syndrome is unfortunate but, until there's a cure, at least it's nice to know that there are positive steps you can take to minimize its effects.

College

"How can I ensure that our baby is accepted by the college of his or her choice?"

By the second month, the initial feelings of joy and/or panic will have worn off, and the time comes for reflection. While your wife isn't even showing, the seismic shift in life is impossible to ignore. Expecting a child is a wondrous, joyful, and awe-inspiring experience. With conception came a rush of new feelings, among them an overwhelming sense of responsibility. Parents-to-be not only need to tend to their babies' health and well-being but also need to educate them, instill pride in them, and most of all, give them every possible edge on the competition.

Smart parents know that. Smart parents know, for example, *when* to give birth, that is, which times of the year will allow their child to avoid those unfortunate school-year "cusps" that ensure that the child is either the very oldest or very youngest in their class.

If you didn't think of that, it's water breaking under the bridge. But don't let another opportunity pass you by. Preparation begins in the womb. If you wait until your baby is born to begin the educational process, they'll probably be okay, just a few steps behind the other kids. What to do? Don't let your fetus spend nine months staring at the uterine walls! Here are just a few ideas:

- *Womb tunes.* All parents play Mozart to their developing fetus. Avoid the clichés and broaden the baby's musical palette. Any classical music is appropriate, with the possible exception of Wagner. If you are less interested in your child's depth of knowledge, and more interested in ensuring that he is considered cool, you could choose to play Dylan, Lou Reed, Ry Cooder, and blues guitar legends such as Albert King and the Reverend Gary Davis. Just don't forget, when those cool kids become teenagers, they hate their parents. Maybe a slightly nebbishy teenager is what you want. To that end, the most sensible approach is to begin with Gregorian chants and other early music, and work chronologically through baroque all the way to the work of such modernists as Copland and John Cage. This will give your unborn child a sense of the historical continuity and development of musical composition.
- *Talk to your womb.* Social skills are just as important as cognitive ones. Make small talk. Establish a sense of propriety and decorum. Speak

firmly, with conviction, but offer support. Remember, love and limits. Kids—and fetuses (feti?)—may test you, but they want to know that you are confident and in charge.
- *Buy the right toys for the fetus.* The Press 'n' Play Alphabet, for example, is a wonderful learning tool. These hand-carved wood letters can be pushed against Mommy's tummy to allow the baby-to-be to begin recognizing his letters.
- In addition to the basic repertoire of literary books on tape, there are also many instructive motivational tapes specifically for the unborn. We especially recommend *Fetus Self-Improvement: Being Born Is Just the Beginning!* which provides gentle music imbued with simple, almost subliminal messages that will make for a better baby: "Don't cry too much," "When it is dark outside, we sleep," and "Let's make toilet-training a priority."

LUCKY GUESSES

"I walk into the office one morning, and a female co-worker takes one look at me and says, 'Is your wife pregnant?' I was so flabbergasted, there was no point in trying to lie—the truth was obvious."

It is traditional not to tell anyone about a pregnancy until the first trimester is safely under your belt, so to speak, but women's intuition waits for no man. You simply weren't prepared. Every pregnant father should be aware that women's intuition is incredibly powerful, and also quite random. It could be your boss, it could be a co-worker, it could be a woman who hardly knows you at all, but at some time—maybe even before you're even sure that your wife is pregnant—they will ask. Be prepared, stay cool, and *lie*. Your wife is depending on you. Think about it: How are you going to explain that after two months of hiding it from all of your nearest and dearest, you went ahead and told Kerrie in accounts receivable?

Chapter Five

The Third Month

What Your Wife Will Be Complaining About

- Exhaustion

- You

- Excessive salivation (medically known as ptyalism, but don't let her try to say it)

- Her weight

- Your weight

- Indigestion

- Indigestion tablets, which make her nauseated

- That she's still dying to tell everyone she's pregnant, but is now convinced that people have guessed

- That nights are not as long as they used to be

- That not knowing the baby's gender makes it impossible to paint and furnish the nursery, or buy clothes, or lock down a name

- These lists, which are demeaning, sexist, and incomplete

- Morning sickness

- No morning sickness, so something must be wrong

- She's seen every rerun of *Sex and the City*

- That aspirin and ibuprofen are good drugs, such nice, friendly, headache-curing drugs—how could they be bad for your baby?

- These prenatal vitamins are so large she needs to eat them with a knife and fork

- That *American Baby* and *Parenting* magazines are still not as interesting as *Vogue* and *Elle*

- Or that *American Baby* and *Parenting* now hold her interest more than *Vogue* and *Elle*, and it scares her

- Emotional highs and lows, fear, ecstasy, anxiety, and elation, often all at the same time, and it scares her

A Couple of Things to Say to Let Her Know You're Caring, Sensitive, and Up on the Required Reading

1. "Isn't it great to know that right now the placenta is beginning to produce its own progesterone, taking over the function of the corpus luteum?"

2. "You know, the danger of Rh sensitization occurs only when an Rh-negative woman is pregnant with an Rh-positive child—and a simple dose of Rh immunoglobulin soon after delivery will prevent the dangerous antibodies from forming. Honey, are you asleep?"

What to Buy This Month

You've got a lot of basics in the closet already, so now you can feel free to purchase actual toys, but don't get behind on the necessities. Buy, buy, buy, and don't look back. Look, there is even a chain of stores called "Buy Buy Baby." What other product category could get away with such an unapologetically blatant sales pitch of a name? "Spend Spend Women's Fashions?" I don't think so. But when it comes to outfitting nurseries, the marketers know that you need to spend, you want to spend, you're going to spend. You just don't feel right until you know some purchase has been made that will meet every possible need your baby may, or may not, someday have.

ESTIMATED COSTS, MONTH THREE
Basics: $880
Basic plus extras: $2,595

Basics
Baby book
Bathtub seat
Blankey
Blocks
Cigars that announce "It's a Boy" or "It's a Girl" (or bubble gum cigars)
Coloring books
Comb for untangling hair
Crib bumper
Crib pad (under sheet)
Duplos (bigger version of Legos), especially that great zoo set
Hair detangler comb
Knee pads for crawling
Musical pull toys
Rubber ducky
Shampoo eye shield
Video camera
(Do not buy a Jack-in-the-box—

What Your Wife May Look Like

At the beginning of the third month, the fetus inside your wife is distinctively human, with a large head, small rump, and fully formed toes and fingers. Though your wife can't feel it, the fetus is now active: it is kicking, clenching and unclenching its fists, pressing its lips together, frowning, and making other facial expressions—and so is your wife, as a matter of fact.

though classic, these are terrifying and emotionally traumatizing toys until the age of ten or so)

Extras

BB gun

Legos (not for the baby, for you, but justified as "an investment for the future")

Model train (same)

Tinkle Targets—floatable bull's-eyes for teaching little boys to aim (or make your own by sketching appropriate targets on toilet paper)

Video-editing software

Wide-angle lens for digital camera

500GB external hard drive to store pictures

WHAT YOU MAY BE CONCERNED ABOUT

Varicose Veins

Q. *"I'll be honest. I think varicose veins are gross. I'd take stretch marks over them any day. Is there anything to do to prevent them?"*

A. To help your wife avoid varicose veins and other circulation disorders, put two- or three-inch wood blocks under the foot end of your bed. A slightly tilted bed will help balance out the effects of daylong gravity.

An interesting side effect of the tilted bed is adnogginal circulation. All the blood rushes to your head, and you may have especially vivid dreams. If you have a severe case, you may have what is known scientifically as "tomato head." If this is the case, you probably have the bed at too steep an angle.

Any efforts on your part to make use of this slightly off horizontal to add a touch of novelty to your evenings are attempted solely at your own risk.

Boy or Girl?

"Everyone we meet seems to have a very definite idea whether we're having a boy or a girl, based on how my wife is carrying, or her complexion, or the alignment of Jupiter and Mars. The remarkable thing is that they all seem to be so sure. Is there any truth to all these old wives' tales?"

Old wives can be a real problem. Take mine . . . please! Irrelevant kidding aside, almost everyone has an ultrasound or two nowadays, so if you want to know, just find out! But there are many other old-fashioned methods that don't involve covering your wife's belly with goop and prodding her with metal instruments. For those who would rather stick with some form of intuition, here are a few of the more popular old wives' tales:

- The faster the heartbeat, the more likely it's a girl.
- Carrying high and long means a boy; low and wide means a girl.
- Easy pregnancies are boys; difficult

ones, girls. No comment.
- If you put on a lot of weight where you sit, it's a girl.
- Food cravings mean boys; chocolate cravings mean girls.
- Italian old wives believe that if you go for the heel of a loaf of bread, it's a boy.
- A clear complexion means a girl; a poor complexion means a boy. But girls will cause more headaches during their adolescence, so it all evens out.
- Pump some stereophonic Motown into the womb. Girls "dance" to music; boys go to sleep. This holds true up to and including junior high school.
- Smooth hands mean a girl; rough hands mean a boy; dry, scaly hands mean you should be doing the dishes for your wife more often.
- When the mother gains weight, you're having a baby, but when Dad gains weight? He's having too many helpings.
- A dream about trying to pick out a prettier postage stamp means it's a girl; a dream in which you really don't want to stop to ask directions means it's a boy.

Her Food Cravings

"My wife still hasn't sent me out to get pickles and ice cream. Is something wrong?"

She will. Some supposedly well-researched, ridiculously best-selling guides to pregnancy have stated that craving pickles and ice cream is just another old wives' tale. They could not be more wrong. Craving pickles and ice cream is an indisputable fact of modern-day pregnancy. Fathers shouldn't feel intimidated or uncomfortable about it. To help expectant fathers serve the very best pickles-and-ice-cream combinations to their wives, we offer some suggestions:

As a general rule, the saltier pickles are best with the deeper flavors of ice cream: the various chocolates—Ultra-Fudge Chunk, Heavenly Hash, Dark Chocolate Thunder—as well as pistachio, coffee, and cookie crunches.

For the exotics—curry pickles and senfgurken—we recommend one of the lighter sorbets. To complement the robust flavor of kosher dills, nothing is quite so perfect as peach ice cream. Chowchow pickles, of course, are a natural with chocolate chip. Mint Oreo was positively made to be served up with baby gherkins. Finally, short brine bread-and-butter pickles go best with a simple vanilla.

"We're hip urbanites, and this whole pickles-and-ice-cream concept seems very passé. Isn't there something more fashion-forward that my wife can crave?"

While pickles and ice cream is classic, there are no limits to the foods a pregnant woman can suddenly demand at two A.M. A longtime vegetarian friend of ours suddenly had to have a ham sandwich late one evening. These nouveaux cravings can be just as pressing, and twice as difficult to satisfy, as the traditional one. Does your 24-hour store carry pasta salad with sun-dried tomatoes? Marinated organic baby corn? Soy-carrot muffins? Find out *before* you start making foolish promises while you're pulling on your shoes and pants. There is no more lonely feeling than cruising the darkened storefronts knowing that if you don't come home with strawberry-rhubarb pie, you might as well not come home at all.

Telling

"We've been dying to tell people that we're pregnant, but now that we can, we're not sure what the best way to go about it is."

The end of the third month, when the odds of miscarriage drop significantly, is the traditional moment to tell the whole world, "We're pregnant!" But how? And whom?

Chances are, your wife has already told her best friend and mother. (Do you get to pick a couple of trusted friends? No, *your* friends cannot be trusted.) If you haven't told the grandparents-to-be, they are surely first on your list, and not just because of familial proximity. It's good to start with people who will express nothing but unbridled joy and happiness. Unless your parents are still harboring severe doubts about your chosen mate, or severe misperceptions about their own age, grandkids are the best news they could hear.

The rest of the phone calls are up to you. The priorities are siblings, close friends, and people you bet that you would get pregnant first. When you start getting bored with "Guess what?" as an opening gambit, get creative. There are plenty of ways to break the news: "How many grandkids do you have . . . so far?" or "I know something you don't know." "We did it!" has an interesting double-entendre.

Whom to tell? The basic rule of thumb is that people should have some sense of who you are, before they are informed that you are expecting. But even here, you should decide what is right for you. If it seems important, then by all means let toll collectors, waitresses, and telemarketing representatives in on your joyous news.

One word of legitimate practical advice before you make your calls: The first natural question in response to your announcement is "When are you due?" (Unless a more natural question is "Are you going to get married?" Or possibly, "Are you two out of your minds?") When people ask when you are due, add two weeks to the actual due date your doctor provided and tell everyone— even your nearest and dearest friends and relatives—*that* is your due date. Why lie? First of all, the date is nothing but an educated guess. More important, during the final month, especially if you are actually late, you will both be going insane, thanks to people saying, "Have you had it yet?" "When was your due date again?" and "Haven't you had that baby yet?" As if you hadn't noticed that your due date had come and gone. The phone calls from folks "just checking in" accelerate as the due date approaches. When you call home, the first words out of your mouth have to be "No baby! Hi, Mom, it's me, just calling to . . ."

Why start all that any earlier than necessary?

Chapter Six

The Fourth Month

What Your Wife Will Be Complaining About

- Exhaustion

- You

- That all the other women in the ob-gyn's waiting room are further along

- That her breasts continue to enlarge, and it ain't over till it's over

- Leukorrhea (we don't want to talk about it)

- Increase in appetite for foods she can't have

- Mild edema, a swelling of the feet, ankles, and cell phone coverage charges

- Parents and friends, who were too excited, not excited enough, or just didn't say the right things when she told them

- That you told people she wanted to tell first

- That books insist that various strange syndromes are incredibly rare, when she's quite sure she has them

- Increased sexual desire or total loss of sexual appetite (no, you don't get to choose)

- The size of your home or apartment

- That she just realized there are recessive genes for red hair on both sides of the family and she isn't sure she will be able to bond fully with a red-haired baby

- That her regular clothes are uncomfortable, but she still is unwilling to commit to pregnancy clothes

- That books promised, they *promised* that morning sickness would end, but you're not being supportive because you don't think her case will hold up in court

- Emotional highs and lows, fear, ecstasy, anxiety, and elation, often all at the same time

A Couple of Things to Say to Let Her Know You're Caring, Sensitive, and Up on the Required Reading

1. "Did you know that right now our baby's sebaceous glands are producing sebum, which mixes with skin cells to form the vernix? Vernix! *Our* baby's vernix."

2. "Diuretics to stop water retention—though still prescribed by some doctors—have been shown to be useless and in fact harmful during pregnancy, causing nutritional deficiencies, fatigue, depression, insomnia, and damage to the kidneys. And Dianetics—don't even go there!"

3. "Oligohydramnios is the condition of having too little fluid in the amniotic sac, whereas polyhydramnios is the condition of having too much. Thank goodness you've got just-right-hydramnios!"

What to Buy This Month

With the passage of the first trimester, the risk of miscarriage is mostly past. Now it is time to forget about the little trinkets and start bringing home the big-ticket items.

ESTIMATED COSTS, MONTH FOUR

Basics: $1,672
Basics plus extras: $2,082

Basics
Baby-size shoehorn
Dora the Explorer home videos and
    licensed apparel
Changing table/dresser
Crayola crayons, in the 64-color box
Crazy straws
Crib
Crib mirror
Food grinder
Glow-in-the-dark stars to stick on
    nursery ceiling
High chair
High chair cushion
Hip-sling baby carrier
Jug of Desitin
The Wiggles CDs (yes, you have to)
Snugli (rhymes with ugly, fittingly)
Spoons shaped like airplanes
Stroller

Extras
Home sonogram machine—why wait
    for an appointment?
Baby Jogger, so baby can have a smooth
    ride while you take a run; or hang on

What Your Wife May Look Like

The fourth month includes that wonderful moment in between the green, morning sickness tones of early pregnancy and the pale, drawn complexion of late pregnancy—yes, the famous "healthy glow." Catch it if you can. Although this is the period when most people make their pregnancy public, your wife will still be dressing in the loose shirts and stretch pants known as basic denial wear. She's trying to achieve the "you're hardly showing" look.

Or . . . she could be of the "dying to show off my pregnancy" school. In that case, she may actually develop a swayback accentuating her small rounded belly, what the celebrity tabloids have taken to calling a "bump." She will wear all-out maternity clothes, modeling each outfit for you, pulling the fabric back to ensure that the abdomen is not lost in the folds. (Don't point this out; just say pregnancy becomes her, or she's glowing, or something like that.)

the garage wall as a nifty device for gathering dust

Retro Slot Car Racing set, so you can recapture your youth and then share it with Baby

Saint Bernard dog, with brandy dram, to come to your rescue

WHAT YOU MAY BE CONCERNED ABOUT

Public Displays of Affection

"Now that my wife is obviously showing, our pregnancy feels so public. I know it's probably ridiculous, but I keep thinking that people will know that we 'did it.'"

Yes, that is ridiculous. Your feelings are silly and wrong. Nonetheless, if you are uncomfortable about this public display of your sexuality, one simple solution would be to tackle the issue head on. If strangers nod and smile, tell them immediately that you only "did it" once, and it wasn't even that much fun. This straightforward approach will make everyone feel much more comfortable about you and your pregnancy. It will get rid of the proverbial "elephant in the room"—so to speak. Better yet, when you sense public disapproval, confront the people who are lifting eyebrows and explain quietly, calmly, and in simple but clear language how a man and a woman make a baby. This may not make everyone comfortable, but at least you will all know what happened. And it's good practice for later.

Am I a Sexist?

"Lately my wife calls me a sexist more and more. I may not be a card-carrying member of NOW, but I was never 'the enemy' before. Is it something about pregnancy that brings out this issue?"

Indeed, pregnancy is a phenomenon so patently unfair to women that it often causes a rising stridency in their responses to any and all gender-related issues. However, avoiding the trap of being dubbed a sexist—and having no

defense—is easy if you follow a few simple rules. Stick to the guidelines below, and you'll have plenty of ammunition the next time she calls you a soulless troglodyte.

- Try to cut down on your use of the expression "chickie baby."
- Watch an Oxygen talk show and pretend to like it.
- Use those Sacagawea and Susan B. Anthony dollars. They're handy once you get used to them.
- Stop arguing that figure skating and gymnastics are not really sports.
- Watch the NCAA Final Four in women's basketball, too.
- Actually read some of the articles in *Glamour* or *Elle* while you're scanning them for babes.
- The next time something needs to be fixed around the house, offer to fix dinner while she does the repair. And pray she says no.
- Even if you mean it as a compliment, never bark at a woman.

Part of the issue may be that, with the complicated task of parenting bearing down on you, so to speak, your wife may be anxious that your inveterate sexism will lead you to create unnecessary gender distinctions in your children. However, you'll find that politically correct gender neutrality is on the wane. It peaked somewhere back in the 1970s—possibly during the airing of Marlo Thomas's TV special *Free to Be . . . You and Me*. Essentially, the feminists won all the major battles, and the last few skirmishes have become less and less mainstream. Today, very few parents will deny that girls are genetically encoded to enjoy wearing tulle and tiaras, and that even the smallest boys cannot resist flinging objects down stairs just to see how much noise they make. This means that you can decorate the nursery in blue or pink, rather that a neutral yellow or green. (Unless you're not finding out the gender before he/she is born—and want to do the nursery beforehand. Green is nice.)

The Ring

"My wife has removed her wedding band. I don't know exactly what she's planning, but I like it here. Should I ask her about it or just wait until I find my stuff outside the front door?"

Relax. Your wife is undoubtedly taking a simple precautionary measure to avoid discomfort when edema (swelling) affects her hands. Shoes, belts, watchbands—everything must be adjusted. In the old days, doctors prescribed a low-salt diet to prevent this water retention—but we now know that some salt is necessary. A pregnant woman's increased blood capacity simply requires a bit of stretching all around. Of course, it is also perfectly normal not to have swelling, so it may well be that your wife has cashed in the jewelry in preparation for the day she hits the road and leaves you crying in your beer. Has she bought a motorcycle lately?

Faking Couvade

"My wife is now convinced that since I haven't experienced any symptoms of couvade syndrome—sympathetic pregnancy—that I'm not sympathetic to her plight. Should I fake it?"

You may have to. (After all, she probably has been faking it now and then to spare your feelings.) Once her mind is made up, there will be no point in quoting statistics about the rarity of the syndrome. You'll have to complain about your swollen feet, absentmindedly rub your belly, drink milk, and pretend to throw up every morning. But there are two other approaches you may want to try first.

The first approach was developed by Dr. Rickard Grolsch in his ongoing Princeton Institute studies on male response theory. His advice is to point out to her that from a psychological viewpoint, most couvade victims are not sympathetic but jealous. *Sympathetic pregnancy* is a misnomer and gives too much credit to men who are selfishly trying to co-opt the pregnancy for themselves. You are a well-balanced, appropriately empathetic person—a helpmate and friend—who understands that the burden of pregnancy, along with its joys, will always be the woman's, first and foremost.

If that doesn't work, you may want to try a more general response strategy developed by a team of Northwestern University relational psychologists led by Dr. Wilma Krobb. They recommend that, rather than directly attack any tender issue, the husband simply make an absurd statement and then defend it vociferously. This is a much more advanced system than Grolsch's, though it is, of course, based on his ground-breaking treatise, "Changing the Subject."

Krobb et al. recommend you begin by speculating that the guppies in the fish tank seem to be depressed. The researchers note that the key to success in this strategy is to insist that this is not a casual joke but a terrifying reality. It may seem at first to increase your wife's ire but, if you persist, she will eventually forget what she was complaining about. Other possible themes: "A stranger has been in the house," "I suddenly put the pieces together and realized my old college roommate isn't who he says he was," "I keep smelling things from the past."

The worst case is that you will actually induce a psychotic episode and will need professional help to escape the personal demons you have unleashed. Actually, that is a pretty bad worst case, isn't it? Well, sometimes drastic measures are called for when you *really* don't want to start a tiff with the wife.

Chapter Seven

The Fifth or Sixth Month—
Somewhere Around There

What Your Wife Will Still Be Complaining About

🪰 Exhaustion

🪰 You

🪰 Absentmindedness

🪰 Fetal movement, not enough or too much

🪰 Breast changes, heaviness, fullness, tenderness, tingling, darkening of the areola

🪰 Your interest in the above

🪰 Absentmindedness. Oh yeah, she already complained about that.

🪰 Backaches, side aches, leg aches, fingernail aches

🪰 That the eleven o'clock news is too scary

🪰 That food cravings are your body's way of telling you what nutrients it needs, so there must be something necessary in chocolate

🪰 Mild edema, or a swelling, of the feet, and "mild" is all it takes to make all her shoes, except the ratty slippers, painful to wear

🪰 That Baby's hiccups have stopped being cute

🪰 People stealing the name she wanted to use, and now she can't possibly use it because every other baby has it and the whole point was that she didn't want a trendy name

🪰 That she has finished reading all the pregnancy books; now she needs new sources of anxiety

🪰 A recurrent need to feel her tummy

🪰 That friends and acquaintances need to feel her tummy

🪰 Emotional highs and lows, fear, ecstasy, anxiety, and elation, often all at the same time

A Couple of Things to Say to Let Her Know You're Caring, Sensitive, and Up on the Required Reading

1. "Your complexion looks fine, honey, but if you're worried about it you might want to try a vitamin B_6 supplement of twenty-five to fifty milligrams—which can help alleviate hormone-related skin blemishes."

2. "Stanislavsky's acting techniques—which involve awareness of the different sets of muscles in the body—can be applied to preparation for childbirth. Perhaps you could have an improvisational birth?"

What to Buy This Month, Whatever Month It Is

In the rush to buy all the stuff at the toy and baby furniture stores, you've probably overlooked all the little basics you'll need from the local pharmacy. Stock up now, and save on errands later.

ESTIMATED COSTS, THE MIDDLE MONTHS
Basics: $419
Basics plus extras: $529

Basics
Alphabet and number refrigerator
  magnets
Backpack carrier
Baby bath
Baby lotion
Baby oil

Baby powder
Baby shampoo
Baby toothbrush
Bassinet (no, it's not a musical
  instrument; ask your wife)
Humidifier
Mechanical swing
Playpen
Portacrib: a travel crib
Walker

Extras
Personalized child-size pool cue
Safety scissors (great for craft projects
  later; great for your clumsy pregnant
  wife now)

What Your Wife May Look Like

The belly can be denied no longer, and with it comes True Maternity Wear from such haute couture labels as La Stork, Dressing for Two, and Preggers of London. Seemingly overnight facial expression and general complexion have gone from "the joy of pregnancy" to "I've been pregnant forever."

Sex During Pregnancy

Q. *"My wife has been, well, sexually hungry just when I'm feeling kind of ambivalent about this odd new body of hers. I've heard this is not unusual, but I don't want to make love that much. Plus, I worry about hurting the baby."*

A. Fear of hurting the baby is a very good "sensitive male" response to your wife's constant sexual demands, but it's far from the only excuse at your disposal. Try: anxiety about burgeoning paternal responsibilities, headache from fine print in pregnancy guidebooks, pulled a muscle constructing the crib, or the "thought we could quit after it worked" argument. If the pressure does not relent, your last, cruel resort is to hint at the unattractiveness of the beached-whale look. Don't take this step without first thinking long and hard about whether you can deal with the repercussions. Remember, you might someday want to do "it" again.

Diapers and Landfills

Q. *"I've heard that diapers are an environmental disaster, and I'm not quite sure how they are causing the polar ice caps to melt, but in any case, is there anything I can do to be more responsible?"*

When the first edition of this book was published in the early 1990s, there was still an active debate between those who swore by disposables and those who believed that cloth diapers were the environmentally conscientious choice. No more. The diaper debate is all but over. Cloth diapers? You might as well suggest that you telegram the grandparents or hire a wet nurse. Disposables are the only choice today, unless you live in a geodesic dome four hundred miles from the nearest signs of civilization.

Perhaps that's overstating the case. There are still outposts on the web of the militant pro-diaper junta. There are indeed still cloth diapers and pinless Velcro diaper covers, yours to be purchased if you feel that only natural cotton is good enough for your baby's bum. In fact, there are legitimate arguments on both sides of this issue.

Users of cloth diapers almost all employ a "diaper service" to clean and supply these all-cotton nappies. So the trucking, chemical cleansing, and production of cloth diapers somewhat undermine the efforts to be "green."

Therefore, the highly convenient, unbelievably absorbent modern disposable diaper is yours to use and love. Or so say all the discussions of ecologically friendly products in parenting and baby magazines. On the other hand, are those magazines likely to go out on a limb and claim that cloth diapers are better—or even a legitimate option—when the bulk of their advertising comes from Pampers, Huggies, and the rest?

If you like the convenience of disposables but are still intent on staying as all-natural as possible, there a few companies that sell versions of the disposal diaper that use fewer chemicals and less plastic. According to reports, they work just about as well, with the only downsides being that they cost a bit more and, for most people, have to be ordered online and shipped.

You could probably do just as much good for the environment by skipping a few changes. Those things can absorb six gallons of liquid and if you don't believe it, take a kid swimming in one. Or you could potty-train at nine months like they do in third-world countries. Apparently the trick is just to carry the kid around with you all the time, naked. Eventually, you'll learn to spot the signs that the baby is about to go. Sounds more like parent training than potty training, but if you've got the time—go for it. No one ever regretted that they didn't change more diapers. (Funny, no one ever suggests teaching infants to use a litter box. Being as they like playing with sand, that would seem a natural.)

The author has actually had personal experience with both cloth and disposable. They were both okay. The kids were equally blasé about running around the house with a full load. But the biggest factor in moving from cloth to disposable was a short conversation I had almost two decades ago with a local diaper service. (We join the conversation in progress.)

AUTHOR: But we returned all seventy diapers, and you only dropped off fifty.

SERVICE: If your standing order is for seventy, then a hundred and forty diapers are in circulation.

AUTHOR: Yes, but I promise you we aren't hoarding diapers, but need seventy delivered.

SERVICE: Are you double-diapering?

AUTHOR: Uh, yes, at night.

SERVICE: Make sure to separate them when you put them in the pail.

AUTHOR: Separate them?

SERVICE: When they spread out the diapers to be counted on the conveyor through the electric eye, the people who separate them sometimes miss some if they're stuck together.

AUTHOR: Oh.

SERVICE: Is there anything else we can help you with? Sir? Hello?

AUTHOR: Oh . . . uh, good-bye.

SERVICE: Bye.

Yes, there are people somewhere who go in to work every Monday morning and take their place at an assembly line where they separate dirty diapers for an electric eye. Think about that the next time you see your wife squinch up her nose and call out, "It's your turn." And if choosing disposables means there is one less fully employed diaper separator in the world, I can't help but feel that is ultimately a good thing.

Becoming a Father

Q "Just being pregnant has meant so many changes in our lifestyle, our planning, our relationship. The prospect of fatherhood is beginning to terrify me."

A Having a child will mean changes, no doubt about it. Along with the great joy and satisfaction that the baby will bring into your home come limitations, sacrifices, and worries. You should prepare by tapering off. You don't want to go cold turkey. Adjusting now to just a few of the deprivations to come will make the initial shock of fatherhood that much easier. Here are ten simple ways to get ready.

1. Stop seeing movies in the theater. Young parents only see movies at home, so if you don't stop going out to the movies now, there will be an awkward lag of six to eight months during which every new release is a movie you've already seen. Netflix can help.

2. Explore additional take-out options. You'll want more choices than pizza and Chinese when you're eating it every night of the week.

3. Check out the late-night television schedule. Sadly, much of basic cable is swamped with paid programming of dubious quality. So unless you're interested in getting involved in buying real estate or the antics of college girls on spring break, you might want to invest in Tivo or the like. With a few favorite shows on queue, you might actually look forward to those two A.M. feedings.

4. If your wife can't get to sleep, drive her around the block seventeen times and then carry her back into the house.

5. Go to the drugstore and say loudly, and without shame, "Excuse me, where are the wipes?" And while you're at it you might as well buy a few now. For a very different challenge, go into a local bar and say loudly, "Excuse me, where are the wipes?"

6. If you smoke, try doing it secretly in the garage. Do it barefoot, too. The cold cement adds to the effect. Don't put it out with your foot, though, and don't forget to pick up the butts *and* the spent matches.

7. Slice a hot dog into ten sections, then cut each circle into choke-proof quarters, and allow them to cool and dry out for one hour. Finally, eat the whole thing yourself because the kid wasn't interested. Use a spoon to add to the challenge.

8. Practice holding your breath for two minutes and seventeen seconds (the amount of time a skilled parent takes to handle a particularly foul diaper change—or, as some call it, a "six-wipe" change).

9. Buy yourself clothes that are too small, then pack them in boxes, carefully label them, store them, and forget about them forever. It may seem pointless, but so are bathrobes for one-year-olds, and we own two.

10. Carry a ten-pound sack of sugar everywhere you go, to build upper-body strength.

Taking the Pledge

Q. "I'm trying to support my wife by joining her in giving up smoking, drinking, and coffee, but it's driving me crazy."

A. It's great to be supportive, and your wife will find your temperance admirable. She will feel that you are working as a team, and also she won't have to face temptation from your cigarettes, martinis, or French roast. If you can do it,

Godspeed, O Perfect Husband!

We recommend another approach. Since your wife can't drink or smoke and may be cutting back on caffeine, you should think of yourself as smoking for two and drinking for two. If she can eat for the baby and for herself, surely you can order a double and drink a toast to your better half!

And by the way, here's the good news: The day your wife found out she was pregnant, she became your designated driver for the next year. It's a handy thing, too, because you could use a drink.

Pregnancy and Childbirth in TV Land

What is the father's role in pregnancy? The answer leaps to mind: to pace back and forth in a waiting room, looking exhausted, then be joyful and flustered with the news, and finally be well meaning but incompetent at handling the baby. Where does your image of this ideal of fatherhood come from? TV land, that magical place where life sure is complicated, but every problem is solved in under half an hour and nobody really gets hurt.

To better understand our own perceptions about childbirth and pregnancy, we must understand where those perceptions came from. The answer, for better or worse, is television. Only by examin-

ing the "myths" and ideals of fatherhood from the small screen can we begin to understand ourselves.

CAREER WOMAN: When *Get Smart*'s Agent 99 and Max finally tied the knot—even before the twins were born—she gave up her career for him: "I found that there just weren't enough hours in the day to be an efficient housewife and a good spy."

CAREER WOMAN, PART II: Lucille Ball surely pulled off the ultimate juggle of career and family when, on January 19, 1953, she gave birth both onscreen and off. Little Ricky was born on *I Love Lucy* on the same day that Lucille Ball, via cesarean, gave birth to Desi Arnaz, Jr. The cover of *TV Guide* and huge ratings resulted.

CIGAR-PASSING: When Ted Baxter finally gave birth—with Georgette's help—the normally ungenerous newscaster from *The Mary Tyler Moore Show* was effusive: "I'm a daddy, I'm a daddy—have a cigarette."

DIAPERS: When *All in the Family*'s Archie Bunker had grandson Joey, the network censors did not want him to be seen changing Joey's diapers. The show resisted and shot the scenes, from discreet angles, of course—and American television had a new first.

DRINKING DURING PREGNANCY: Worried about drinking during your pregnancy? It is best to avoid drinking, but remember that our mothers drank and smoked all pregnancy long, and it may not have been good for us, but we survived. There is an episode of *Bewitched* that underscores the attitudes of an earlier era. Mrs. Tate (Darrin's boss's wife) is anxious about telling her husband Larry that she just found out that she is pregnant. Samantha helps her overcome her anxieties by giving her a pep talk and by pouring her numerous martinis. Of course, due to an overheard conversation, Larry and Darrin arrive under the mistaken impression that Samantha is the one who is pregnant and keeping it a secret. The episode is rarely shown in syndication because of the martinis.

DRIVING: The main focus of many pregnant fathers in TV land is the drive to the hospital. Their responsibility begins with the first pangs of labor and ends when their wife is safely delivered to the hospital. After that it's all pacing. Rob Petrie on *The Dick Van Dyke Show* lay in bed fully dressed and, in a famous bit, practiced leaping and putting on his hat in one quick motion to slice a few tenths of a second off that all-important car trip. When Agent 99 was expecting the twins, Maxwell Smart spent most of his time figuring out the fastest possible route to the hospital. Of course, when the time finally came, he accidentally drove right into a Kaos trap—part of an exciting two-parter called "And Baby Makes Four."

PAIN RELIEF: Did Samantha Stevens consider using magic to spare herself the pain of labor and childbirth? The *Bewitched* episodes surrounding the birth of Tabitha and later Adam are unclear, but judging from her chipper look in the hospital, you can bet she isn't worried about her episiotomy stitches.

Where TV Babies Come From

In the early years of television, birth was discussed only in veiled terms. The word "pregnant," for example, was forbidden. As you can imagine, there weren't a lot of jokes about women rupturing their amniotic fluid on the dance floor—we had to wait for *Desperate Housewives* to see that played out. The addition of children to a family was almost always nonbiological in nature.

When Jeff and Mary Stone started getting long in the tooth, for example, Donna Reed added to her brood by adopting Trisha—a little girl who followed them home from the park one day. Try explaining that in terms of birds and bees.

My Three Sons explored both adoption and natural additions. Ernie was adopted when Mike moved out. But Robbie and Katie eventually had the triplets—Steve Jr., Charley, and Robbie II—while Steve, the patriarch, went back to adoption the long way around by marrying Dodie's mother, Barbara.

More Recent, More Racy

Today, TV can tell it like it really is—for better or worse. There may still be a few words you can hear only on cable, but there are certainly no more "storks" in prime time. If you want to prepare for your own baby by reliving the entire eighth season of *Friends*, it is available on DVD. Just remember that, in the labor room, your wife won't have the same hairstylist and makeup artist that Jennifer Aniston had. But certainly, this series has plenty of valuable lessons to offer expectant parents. The Valentine's Day birthing video episode springs to mind. But that turned out to be the least of Monica and Chandler's fertility problems.

Miranda's long, emotionally overwrought pregnancy and childbirth in the fourth season of *Sex and the City* is another option. But the symbolism in Carrie's saying good-bye to Mr. Big while rushing to be by Miranda's side is a little heavy. From a husband's perspective, *Sex and the City* offers few positive role models. You're either an essentially hapless sperm donor, or a compromise choice based on some dream guy disappearing.

A Final Note

As you reexamine television, your wife may doubt that your motives are pure. She may feel that watching so much TV is a waste of time. One way to combat her criticism is to enlist her as a fellow viewer. Tell her, and this is quite true, that in certain segments of the market research done by the Nielsen Ratings, a pregnant woman is statistically considered to be two viewers. It may seem strange but, for the marketers of baby and child care products—diapers, toys, rug cleaners—this is a valid measurement of the impact their television commercials are having, so your wife is, quantitatively speaking, watching for two.

Staying Married

"We both wanted to have this baby but, now that we're pregnant, we just can't seem to get along. She's so moody and unpredictable."

You're not the only person who has to adjust emotionally to having a baby—this period of transition can be hard on your wife, too. And don't forget, she's got all the minor physical discomforts of pregnancy to deal with as well. So be patient, understanding, forgiving, thoughtful. Listen to all her complaints and criticism without being petulant or defensive. Give, give, give. Buy flowers, write poems, and stay home from work, just to take care of her. How can you do it? How can you manage to transform so completely? Simple: by matching every thoughtful act with a passive-aggressive jab. A long, low whistle when she steps on the scale ("It was just a joke, sweetie") or cooking heavily spiced stews, chili, thick pungent soups—there are a hundred little ways to needle your mate, and after a long day of feeling put-upon, coming up with them will be second nature.

A second option is to take the offensive. Start complaining about your day the minute you hit the front door, don't even pause for breath for ten to fifteen minutes, and then say, "Oh, baby, I'm sorry. Going on and on about my troubles. How are you feeling?" She'll either buy it or slug you.

The final remedy is to provide your wife with other outlets for gripping.

Is she talking to her mother often enough? Does she have plenty of other pregnant friends? Do whatever you can to foster these relationships. The more they hear, the less you have to hear. You do run the risk of magnifying her annoyance, if for example, her girlfriend is married to some saintly do-gooder. Generally, you'll be better off if you can encourage her to vent to women of a previous generation. Mom and aunts were in relationships and marriages with men who were relatively Neanderthal compared with modern-day men. If you can't measure up to Uncle Stan in the sensitivity department—there's nothing we can say to help.

Chapter Eight

The Seventh Month

What Your Wife Will Constantly Be Complaining About

- Exhaustion
- You
- Clumsiness, disorientation, headache—it's a bit like being drunk without the tranquility and loss of inhibition
- Shortness of breath, dizziness, heartburn, nasal congestion—it's like smoking without getting to light up
- Strong and frequent fetal movement—and the novelty has worn off
- That she's tired of complaining about the same old symptoms and wants new symptoms
- Itchy abdomen
- High cost (and limited use) of maternity panty hose
- That she always gets called on to demonstrate in childbirth preparation class
- Sciatic nerve problems, which are both painful and difficult to pronounce
- Her company's maternity leave policy
- That your company has never even heard of paternity leave
- That her best friend's ob-gyn sounds nicer than hers
- Her weight
- You haven't even had the baby yet, and there's a "product recall" of one of the things you bought
- You picked now, when she is as big as a house, to go on a little diet and lose ten pounds?
- That people make jokes when she enters elevators
- That medical textbooks (purchased for complete, scientific details of every single possible problem) are expensive and their prose style is tedious
- Nonalcoholic beer, which just doesn't do it
- Just realized that Baby won't arrive in time to be a deduction for the current tax year
- That she doesn't want to know what sex the baby is, but it seems unfair that the doctors know
- That you are halfway through this silly humor book, and you still haven't read any of the real pregnancy books
- Emotional highs and lows, fear, ecstasy, anxiety, and elation, often all at the same time

A Couple of Things to Say to Let Her Know You're Caring, Sensitive, and Up on the Required Reading

1. "You know, they say that vitamin E can be very helpful in preventing varicose veins; of course, I mean vitamin E in the form of d-alpha tocopherol acetane. Mixed tocopherols don't have any effect on varicose veins, naturally."

2. "You can practice the breathing techniques you learn in class by trying to control the pain of a headache, or a stubbed toe. Every little accident is an opportunity."

What to Buy This Month

By now, many pregnant couples will know their baby's gender and so can begin reinforcing sexual stereotypes right from day one, by choosing boy or girl clothes, boy or girl colors for the nursery, and boy or girl careers for which to press.

ESTIMATED COSTS, MONTH SEVEN
Basics: $722
Basics plus extras: $2,490, plus $24.95 per month

Basics
CDs of lullabies
Rearview mirror enhancer, so you can see the backseat
Baby monitors
Baby sweater with fruit motif; or baby sweater with truck motif
Bathtub (infant-size, not regular)
Child-size bathroom sink (fits in tub)
Infant-size party dress or baseball uniform
Juice dispenser
Nightlight
Nursery art
Piggy bank
Rocking chair
Supply of disposable diapers—a couple crates to get started
Teeny-tiny baby fingernail clippers
Travel diaper kit

Extras
All the premium cable TV channels (parents never go out)
Christening gown (if you're Christians)
Dr. Seuss, complete
Tiara or football helmet
Second Tivo (I'm telling you, parents really never go out)

What Your Wife May Look Like

That healthy white glow is now here to stay, and she is too tired to make any sort of facial expression at all. Yes, her breasts are now larger. No, you can't touch them—they're painfully sensitive. She will also stop denying the need to get off her feet, to the point of asking old ladies and war veterans to give up their seats for her.

Let's Be Alarmist

Q. *"Reassurance, reassurance, reassurance. My wife and I are sick of all the books and doctors and friends comforting us and telling us that there's nothing much to worry about. We want to worry."*

A. Most people would like to go through all nine months of pregnancy thinking happy thoughts but, let's face it, you're not really pregnant if you're not going crazy worrying about all the things that could go wrong, feeling guilty about all the little things you may have done wrong, and poring over every new pregnancy and childbirth article in the newspapers and magazines. Paranoia is a perfectly healthy reaction to pregnancy.

We have already promised that this book would not raise unreasonable fears, so we feel honor-bound not to tell you that your tap water may already be limiting your child's intellectual potential; nor will we tell you which brands of coffee use beans sprayed with dangerous pesticides or that too much soy products contain something really bad for you. It would also be wrong for us even to bring up such unlikely disorders as Flander's syndrome, fetopelvic melanoma, or even gestational aneuristic halitosis. Their incidence is so statistically improbable that they are hardly worth mentioning.

Have we piqued your curiosity? That's why the Internet was invented. You are just a high-speed connection away from a virtually unlimited collection of half-truths, misinformation, opinionated speculation, and fringe medical theories. Search for pregnancies gone awry, babies gone crazy, obstetricians gone wild. The dangers of too much tofu or of dying your hair. It's all there. Just steer clear of the well-traveled, professionally designed sites like Babycenter, AmericanBaby, WebMD, or Parenting. What's the fun in getting carefully edited pregnancy and medical information? The crackpots, herbal medicators, and antiestablishment reactionaries are much more interesting.

If you still find that your need for anxiety is outstripping the available Web sites on pregnancy, you might want to start searching for blogs and rants about the sorry state of America's educational system, the effect of television on modern culture, the political history of the Mideast, or the fragility of the ecosphere. And that's just for starters. It's the new Internet six degrees of separation. If there is something out there that just one person is worried about, you can find it within six links.

Sex During Pregnancy

"What exactly are the chances of having sex during pregnancy?"

Sexual relations during this physically and emotionally traumatic period are nothing to worry about. You should remember that the statistical chances of having sex during pregnancy are very low, almost negligible. Odds are, you'll never have to deal with it. Still, every pregnant father worries about it and, yes, it could happen to you. If your thirty-weeks pregnant wife is feeling amorous, don't panic. Yes, she can be an intimidating physical presence, but if you proceed with caution, and don't bring any unrealistic expectations to the process, you may find that you actually enjoy it.

Doing the Lamaze

"Do I really have to take Lamaze classes? Can't I just read a pamphlet for a few tips and just be really pleasant and positive during labor?"

To start with, what were once widely known as Lamaze classes are seldom actually called "Lamaze" anymore. They tend go by more innocent and generic names like Childbirth Preparation or Birthing Readiness. The Lamaze organization seems to have taken a hard-line all-natural approach, and most hospitals don't go for politicizing the process. There was always something a little cult-like about going to a Lamaze class. And who was this Lamaze, anyway? Now it just doesn't matter. But you still have to learn to breathe funny and watch a scary movie or two.

In any case, don't let the prospect of a little tedium and having to hear the words *labia* and *nipple* spoken aloud in public keep you away from class. This is your one chance to do something useful! You're the coach, man, and whether your personal style is more Phil Jackson or Bobby Knight, this is an opportunity to get involved.

Use the classes to get yourself into a childbirthin' frame of mind. The game is tied and going into the ninth inning. It's overtime, gut-check time, and you had better know what all your options are. What will you do if the obstetrician notices a breech condition and calls an audible for a cesarean? What if your wife is clearly tiring, but the anesthesiologist says it's too late for an epidural? If you're going to coach this birth, you'd better have a game plan, and class is the place to get it.

The classes themselves vary greatly from instructor to instructor. The better instructors show a lot of films, go over breathing and relaxation techniques every week, talk a lot about pain, and otherwise provide down-and-dirty preparation. The worst classes start at the very beginning, like a sort of remedial health class. You'll get the charts of the fallopian tubes, the egg and the sperm, even mitosis and meiosis if you're really unlucky. Then they walk you through fetal development, and only get to the breathing gimmicks and "Choices in Pain Relief" in the last meeting or two. The only advantage of this type of class is that they are slightly more likely to give you a small suitable-for-framing diploma in childbirth.

Home Alone

"My wife is considering a home birth. But I don't know, I guess I'm more traditional."

What are you talking about? You're not more traditional, you're more sane. Home birth?! Yeesh! All right, pregnancy isn't a disease, and modern hospital care may be a little dehumanizing and expensive, and skyrocketing malpractice awards make doctors too quick to resort to a C-section. Sure, sure, sure, but those are not reasons to just give up and stay home. Obviously, the hospital has better backup for medical emergencies, but that's just part of it. Do you want to listen to your answering machine picking up right in the middle of active labor? Does your bed at home adjust to seventy-five different positions? Is your television mounted to the ceiling?

Go to the hospital; you'll love it. In fact, more often than not, once she has gotten comfortable, your wife won't want to leave the 24-hour nurse attendants, the adjustable bed with handy swivel tray, and the free, professional babysitting. Only those icky meals and the gentleman from the insurance company will finally urge her out and on her way.

have strange dreams, experience mood swings, and want to pee every half hour. While the staff smoke and drink in front of you, you'll enjoy a smorgasbord of fresh vegetables, whole wheat, bran, iron- and calcium-rich foods, and, of course, pitchers of milk. Finally, you will be asked to pass a greased honeydew melon. No, not really.

Pregnancy Simulations

"My wife says I'm a jerk. While that seems to me to be a rather broad, over-generalized statement, she has suggested that I go to one of these pregnancy-simulation weekends."

It may not be the cure for jerkiness, but a well-managed, professionally run pregnancy simulation weekend can change your attitude about what your wife is going through. The specifics vary but, generally, these camps and spas attempt to approximate the experience of late pregnancy. With cute names like "The Nine-Month Weekend," "A Little Bit Pregnant," and "Daddy's Turn," they offer a variety of programs but follow the same pattern. Naturally, it begins when you strap on a forty- to seventy-pound water-filled "womb." (Your womb is heavier than your wife's because it is in proportion to your body weight—no breaks, mister.) You then ingest some mild drugs, which will make you feel disoreiented, and will

Rubber Baby Buggy Bumpers

"Some acquaintances seem to think that the wife's belly is fair game—they reach over and rub without even asking!"

As the due date approaches, you will find that—much like rubbing the Buddha's belly—it seems to be considered good luck to lay hands on that taut kettledrum that your wife is lugging around. The standard etiquette books offer little advice when it comes to patting other people's bellies. Is it acceptable among relatives? Close friends? Female acquaintances only? In a business setting? While pregnant women will have varying tolerance for the intrusion, most observers agree that, by the eighth month, all pregnant bellies are awfully tempting targets.

The one group of would-be belly rubber that must be turned down definitively is the kind who ask you, not her, for permission, as though you are the proprietor of a traveling freak show.

It may seem difficult to turn down a polite request, but it really isn't. No explanation or diplomacy is necessary. All you need to do is feign complete horror at the suggestion. Furrow your brow and let your mouth drop open, as though they had asked permission to feel your armpit. You could even counter with "No, but I'm concerned I may have a hernia—would you mind having a check?"

If, on the other hand, your wife is *not* shy about sharing her overgrown personal space, and positively wants people to feel the baby kicking, then you might as well charge a couple of bucks. You can probably bump it to five or ten when the baby is kicking. It may seem mercenary, but formula ain't free.

Breast Is Best

"My wife is on the fence about breastfeeding. She's heard all the health arguments, but she can't get used to the idea of it, and is concerned about her figure, etc. What about me? Which is best, from a husband's perspective?"

Public health advocates are increasingly pressing the importance of breastfeeding over formula. For some women, this additional pressure is just one more way they feel pushed around. As usual, our advice is to be "opinion-neutral" for as long as possible. As soon as you become an advocate for one side or the other, you become an easy target.

That said, there are pros and cons. Breastfeeding definitely changes breasts, during the period of breastfeeding, from recreational to functional. But they'll be back. Breastfeeding is cheaper. Breastfeeding is healthier. Do you get the impression that we favor breastfeeding? You're right, and all fathers should. Why? Laziness, my friend. Laziness. When there are no bottles to be sterilized, dried, mixed, and given—well, there's really hardly any reason for *you* to even wake up.

P.S. If she does choose to breastfeed, just remember that at some point when baby is six months old or so, you just go and grab away his favorite toy and stick it in your mouth. When he starts to cry, just say: "See? How do you like it?" It's important to let him know who is boss.

Chapter Nine

The Eighth Month

What Your Wife Will Be Complaining About

- Exhaustion
- You
- How much room you take up in the bed
- Her weight
- Bleeding gums
- That low-sodium food is low-taste
- Unattractive distortion of her belly button
- Strong, uncomfortable fetal movements (new nickname for Fetus: the Karate Kid)
- The distance between the TV and the bathroom
- Braxton-Hicks contractions—if that was one, she doesn't want anything to do with real contractions
- That a month is a very long time
- That you never raise your hand in childbirth class
- Waistbands of maternity pants, where it is unclear whether they go over the belly or under

- Extremely vivid and terrifying dreams
- Numerologist says the due date isn't good
- That you just don't understand
- Somehow NetFlix makes you feel guilty about not watching enough TV
- Hanna Andersson stuff is so much cuter but so much more expensive than Old Navy
- That she really misses sushi
- That you refuse to follow the advice of that other guidebook to call the local authorities to see if they will come by and check your microwave for leakage
- Nicknames you have given her lately (Moby, Barge, Her Hugeness)
- Disorientation and inability to focus—she now consistently loses to you at Boggle
- Emotional highs and lows, fear, ecstasy, anxiety, and elation, often all at the same time

A Couple of Things to Say to Let Her Know You're Caring, Sensitive, and Up on the Required Reading

Remember, unlike much of the information in this book, these are actual facts discovered in the actual reading of other books.

1. "Fetoscopy—which is less common than ultrasound or amniocentesis—allows doctors to photograph the fetus. But it is still primarily experimental, so we don't have to worry about it."

2. "When the baby has the hiccups, it may be because he is actually practicing breathing in the amniotic fluid."

3. "The breathing techniques from childbirth are found in other cultures. The Zulu, for example, teach pregnant women to go to the door of their hut each morning and breathe through each nostril, alternately."

What to Buy This Month

Don't panic! So you're out of money—you can't be out of credit yet. And if you are, start hitting up the grandparents-to-be. After all, they wanted this child as much as anyone.

ESTIMATED COSTS, MONTH EIGHT
Basics: $275
Basics plus extras: $410

Basics
Baby thermometer
Baseball glove
Diaper pail
Frozen dinners
Hooded baby towel
Juice canteen
Nasal aspirator
Stuffed teddy bear
Swaddling blankets
Supply of baby Tylenol
Velcro diaper covers
Washcloths

Extras
Catcher's mitt/first baseman's glove
Clothing with team logos
Clothing with the insignia of the university you expect your child to strive to get into (especially bibs)
Clothing with family crest
Wipes warmer, which electronically warms diaper wipes for easy changes (some models also warm shaving cream)

What Your Wife May Look Like

The eighth month is when the slight waddle appears, especially toward the end of the month. By now she will have gained twenty-five to forty-five pounds and yet look, with her drawn face, as if she is starving. Most of her fashion choices are now made on the basis of how easy they are to deal with when she needs to pee every twenty minutes.

Sex During Pregnancy

"My wife is so big, but she's so happy not to be using birth control that we're having more sex than ever. Are there any limitations we should be aware of in late pregnancy?"

Good for you. Next time, write to *Penthouse*—maybe they'll care. Okay, fine, what was the question again? Oh, yes, limitations. As far as restrictions go, unless your doctor indicates otherwise, a healthy pregnancy should cause no limitations so long as you are both comfortable, with the only exception being that it is important not to blow air into your wife's vagina during oral sex. If this limitation creates a major problem for you, then you know something we don't.

By the way, if you happen to be reading your wife's copy of Vicki Iovine's *The Girlfriend's Guide to Pregnancy* (a popular read that's fairly humane in its treatment of husbands), you may come across the "at the hospital" example, regarding how soon after childbirth some couples start getting frisky again. (No, not intercourse—that's flat out.) Whatever you do, don't point it out to your wife. She saw it and, like every other woman in the world, she understood the story's underlying message: some women are out of their minds.

Fetal Anger

Q. *"My wife has had a lot of discomfort with the baby kicking up a storm. In fact, I'm trying to convince her that he doesn't have a grudge against her. That isn't possible, is it?"*

A. Fetal distress is one thing; fetal emotional distress is another. The first is a physiological problem; the second is a psychological problem—in the mother. Unless you're a strong believer in original sin, or suffer from extreme paranoia (which is not unusual at this stage of pregnancy), it is reasonable to assume the baby holds no grudges. She's not mad at her mother; she's just getting crowded, feeling pressured, and finally kicking back. The same basic process will happen again during adolescence.

The Baby Book

Q. *"We want to make a nice baby book, but everything we've seen is just too adorable for words. What should we do?"*

A. It is handy to have a book that lays it all out for you—from "Your impressions of baby's first moments," "First birthday party," "First words," all the way to "Baby's first act of crummy teenage rebellion." But such books limit your creativity. Scrapbooking is now one of America's most popular hobbies, as well as one of America's newest verbs. Why not make your own? You should decide for yourself what's important, and, in any case, you probably won't get beyond about the second month before the book just becomes a convenient holder for keepsakes that you're going to glue in and annotate "one of these days."

You could just admit defeat from the start and, instead of buying a book, just buy a handsome keepsake box and throw everything into it. Another option is to just keep a few stray notes and wait until the kid is old enough to put it together without your help. It's their book, after all.

You can probably think of all the basic keepsakes, significant moments, and plenty more, but here are a few additional suggestions of things you might have missed:

- ID bracelet from hospital (have you checked it, by the way?)
- Pressed flower from bouquet sent to Mom
- Pressed belly button stump
- Hospital bill (start in on the guilt from day one)
- Newspaper clippings from the day Baby was born: headlines, baseball standings, movie listings, horoscope, weather report, lottery numbers, real estate listing, and oh that "Marmaduke"
- First time Baby was dropped on head and screamed so much it scared the hell out of you

- First bad haircut
- First time Baby hit speed dial on cell phone and called your brother in St. Louis
- First time Baby allowed a hat to stay on for more than two seconds
- First time Baby found television sitcoms predictable (look for this one, generally, at around eighteen months)
- Souvenir shard from the first piece of antique crystal Baby destroyed
- First time a hypnotist convinced Baby to act like a chicken

And why not leave room to encapsulate Baby's whole childhood? After all, they're still your baby until they leave home.

- Baby's first f-bomb
- Baby calls you hypocrite, accurately, for the first time
- Baby's first juvenile offense
- First time Baby goes to Web sites Baby shouldn't have been on
- First time Baby spaces out and forgets to go to college interview
- First time Baby "celebrates" St. Patrick's Day
- You get the idea . . .

The Least Complete Baby Name Guide

James for a boy, and Emma for a girl. There, done. You don't even have to read the rest of this section.

Not good enough, huh? Well, it is true that naming your child is an extremely personal, idiosyncratic process. No two couples go about it the same way. Actually, there were two couples that went about it the same way, but it turned out that each father treasured a broken gold medallion, each was adopted, each married a woman named Helen, and each believe that Steely Dan was an underrated band, but that's another story and a very long one, too. You just want to name your baby.

Naming the baby is a joyful and creative task, but it can be a sincerely awe-inspiring task, too. Naming implies possession, total responsibility. It is the first time that you must see your baby not as a mere miracle of nature, but as a future participant in society. A name gives a child reality, definition, future. The implications are enormous. Names can be traditional—and stereotypical. They can be poetic—and strange. They can bespeak glamour or simplicity, strength or wisdom, multiculturalism or rabid fundamentalism—all in a tiny being who has got a few reflexes, a gnarly fresh belly button, and 20/400 vision. And you thought naming your cat was hard. What are you going to do?

Play it safe and stick to our list. Sure, no one will tell you, "Oh, that's a beautiful name!" but that's okay because when they do say that, what they're really thinking is, "Why do bad names happen to cute babies?" Here are five good names for each sex that may be a little dull, but that's what names should be: safe and innocuous.

Don't waste your cash on some 50,000-name paperback—this is plenty to choose from.

BOYS: Ryan, Joshua, David, Michael, Brian
GIRLS: Madison, Michelle, Sophia, Alexandra, Caitlyn

Of course, we know that you won't take our advice. Days and weeks will be expended in the effort to come up with a name that (a) you both like, (b) isn't already in the top-fifty lists—or top ten, for that matter, and (c) sounds reasonable with your last name. Perhaps the reason that naming has become such a traumatic ordeal is that it serves the perfect, ultimately inconsequential decision to take your mind off all the actual worries surrounding having a baby.

While it is important to create a Web site for your baby as soon as possible, do not let the availability of a domain name influence your choice of their actual name! Do you really want your child named Ethan1168 Jones? Or Elizzzzabeth? Or Chris2pher? Let them pick their own screen name when the time comes.

BONUS BABY-NAMER'S TIP: No matter how thankful you are, don't name the baby Epidural, or even Epi. If you really feel the need to thank the pain reliever, perhaps the name of your anesthesiologist would be a better choice. Best of all, wait a few days. You may find that your extreme appreciation will pass.

What to Name Your Baby When You're Not Serious About Naming Your Baby

It has now been established through genetic mapping that one of the traits linked to the male sex is obsessive joking when faced with the task of naming a baby. Even before the physiological research, field observation had clearly supported the theory. According to 1990 figures, the average pregnant woman found 3.5 joke names amusing, and would laugh politely at roughly 7.7 names; a pregnant father, however, would laugh at up to 78.5 ridiculous names that he himself made up. The disparity is a problem. However, the solution is simple. Men should simply realize that joking about names is to be saved for office and poker-night banter. Women should understand that the urge to make stupid suggestions is almost irresistible. For example, the list below has no real practical purpose except that, as a typical man, the author couldn't resist.

BOYS	GIRLS
Blind Lemon	Bertrude
Dagbert	Duchess
Enos	Tallulah
Fonz	Eccentricia
Fudgie	February
George Foreman VI	Jersey
Itchy	Kermette
Sluggo	Moxie
Pogo	Mylar
The Truth	Petunia
Upchuck	Pip
Walmart	Spaldeen
Zebulon	Corvette
Dacron	Taffeta
Shemp	San Diego
Bladd	Falala
Gillette	Glo-o-o-o-o-oria

Special Revised Edition Baby-Naming Notes

By the way, when this list was first published in the original edition, the name Mercedes was included as a humorous girl's name. Our apologies to the thousands of Americans who disagreed, because Mercedes has actually climbed onto the top 100 American baby names for girls. While we found it absurd in 1992, because it seemed so obviously an automobile and not a person, apparently lots of other parents disagree. Porsche and Ferrari will probably soon make their way onto the real list, so in the meantime I've replaced Mer-

cedes with Corvette. Joke or harbinger? We shall see.

In a related matter, shortly after the original edition of this book was published in the early '90s, publishers in Europe decided to do translations, one in Dutch and another in French. Though delighted by the global attention, we were honestly a bit concerned as to whether the distinctly American cultural references would export. Is Ben & Jerry's a religion among pregnant Dutch women, as it is here? Do French men understand the difficulty of throwing away your baseball cards? Not to mention that the very "expecting" pun upon which this tome rests is apparently not translatable.

Nonetheless, the book was duly translated and *Een Baby Op Komst!* and *Un Bébé Arrive* were published. As an author and monolinguist (no, that's not dirty) with only a smattering of high school French, I nonetheless thoroughly enjoy flipping through both editions. My favorite translated article to ponder is the list of "names to avoid" that appears above.

Apparently, in Holland, they agree that most of the original suggestions are poor choices (though they spell Fonz with an *s*—Fons), but they have replaced the girl's name Duchess with Hertogin and replaced the boys' names The Truth and Upchuck with De Warrheid and Kotsje. Perhaps these are simply literal translations? If so, we remain concerned that perhaps something may have been lost in the translation.

Not so in La Belle France! In this edition, the translator has provided an entirely revised list. Apparently in France, it would be *irrésistiblement drôle* to name a *garçon* Dagobert, Jean-Noël, or Donald. For the *filles*, you should resist the temptation to choose such names as Lolo, Rika, Ghislaine, or Bernarde. Oddly enough, Paulette, Julienne, and Liane also make the list—and they sound like fine names to this American. So be warned, if you plan on taking little Paulette to Paris, the waiters won't only be snobby—thanks to some obscure Gallic reference, they may just giggle at your baby!

It's Just A Dream

Q. *"Lately my wife's dreams have become especially vivid. But when she tells them to me, I am still incredibly bored. Is there something wrong with me?"*

A. Not at all. During the last trimester, a woman's dreams become wilder and will seem frighteningly real to her. Natural anxieties, hormonal changes, and sleep deprivation account for this, but there is nothing more tedious than hearing a dream. "Say, that reminds me of a story that has no particular beginning or end and doesn't make any sense. Care to hear it?" "Oh, sure, honey, just let me know when a character is no longer who they started out as, or when you completely change where you are, okay?"

And if you're thinking that you could try to interpret her dreams symbolically, forget it. First, the chances are good that your effort will make her cry. Second, these dreams are so bizarre that they defy conventional interpretation. Experienced Freudian analysts have been known to hear the dreams of women in the third trimester and say nothing but, "Whoa, that's weird!"

If she or you would still like to have a go at interpretation, use the basic guide on the following page.

What to Dream When You're Dreaming

The dreams of pregnant women—spurred on by hormonal shift, increased blood circulation, and natural anxieties—become incredibly vivid, sometimes frighteningly so. It can be reassuring to understand where these dreams come from, and who better than the husband to play psychologist?

As you do form your analyses, realize that dreams cannot be understood merely as a group of symbols with standardized interpretations. The imagery of dreams has specific, personal meanings that defy simple attempts to classify and demarcate. On the other hand, dreams cannot be understood much at all, so you might as well try our glossary.

Here is your basic dictionary of dream symbols specific to pregnancy. Remember, our interpretations apply only to your wife's dreams. Any attempt to analyze your own dreams according to this chart could lead to hysterical pregnancy. And you don't want one of those.

Symbol/Meaning

BLUE, COLOR
Issues of cognition, or logic, or possibly that it's a boy

CARS
Wish to escape, or wish to move quickly, or wish that you could fit behind your own steering wheel

CROSSING A RIVER
A change in attitude

DIAPERS
Fear of changing diapers

DESERT
Dessert

EATING
Generalized wish fulfillment

FLOATING
Fear that you now resemble a hot-air balloon

FLYING
Fear, specifically, that you now resemble the Sea World blimp

MOUNTAINS
Distant goal, separation

OLD WOMAN
Eternal female wisdom; or, to the contrary, fear that your mother-in-law will come to visit

PARALLEL PARKING
Resentment of having to "back and fill" or even execute difficult "K-turns" to exit from dining rooms of certain local restaurants

STORK
Diaper delivery service

TEST, NOT BEING PREPARED FOR
Fear of labor

TREES
Hammock envy, probably connected to a strong wish to lie down

UNDERWEAR, GOING TO SCHOOL IN YOUR
Fear of same

WHALES
Childbirth class

Chapter Ten

The Ninth Month

What Your Wife Will Be Complaining About

- Exhaustion
- You
- All men
- That if it's false labor, it shouldn't be real pain
- Your weight
- Everything on the "What Your Wife Will Be Complaining About" lists for months one through eight
- That she needs an assistant to read the bathroom scale
- That the bathtub is not deep enough anymore
- That even maternity wear is no longer comfortable; she's down to exactly one dress that can reasonably be said to fit, and she bought that at a drapery store
- Braxton-Hicks contractions
- That a double bed should be a queen; or the queen should be a king; or the king should really be a quarter-acre of firm mattress
- The color you painted the nursery, which now seems too dark
- Mr. Braxton, Mr. Hicks, and their children's children
- When you try to bring her breakfast in bed, the bed table—well, it doesn't quite work anymore
- Not getting a seat on the bus or subway
- Not being able to get up from seat on the bus or subway
- The decor of your home as the nesting instinct kicks in
- Automobile seatbelt now impossible to wear
- The color you repainted the nursery—it's too light
- People who tell her stories of very difficult births
- People who tell her stories of very easy births
- People who tell her stories
- That Baby doesn't seem to know that the due date has passed
- Fear of in-laws sending baby clothes she will hate
- That you really shouldn't be painting inside the house so much; the fumes can't be good for the baby
- Emotional highs and lows, fear, ecstasy, anxiety, and elation, often all at the same time

A Couple of Things to Say to Let Her Know You're Caring, Sensitive, and Up on the Required Reading

1. "While Leboyer childbirth seems appealing, there is no firm scientific evidence to support the arguments made in the book *Birth Without Violence*."

2. "A nonstress test may seem like a pregnancy oxymoron, but it is called that to distinguish it from a stress test, which is essentially the same monitoring of the baby, with the added 'stress' being an oxytocin drip to set off contractions."

What to Buy This Month

The baby's got to eat, right? This is the month to get ready for the bottle or the breast.

ESTIMATED COSTS, MONTH NINE
Basics: Bottle $759, Breast $310
Basics plus extras: Bottle $1,959,
  Breast $1,510

Basics
BOTTLEFEEDING
Automobile bottle warmer (plugs into
  cigarette lighter)
Bottle brush for cleaning
Bottle drying rack
Bottle sterilizing pan
Bottles
Formula
Hypoallergenic formula (just in case)
Rubber nipples

BREASTFEEDING
Book on why breastfeeding is best
Breast pump
Nipple shields
Nursing bras
Nursing pads

BOTH METHODS
Birth announcements
Car seat, up to 25 pounds
Car seat, 25-40 pounds

Extras
Library of works on child rearing
  and education: Jean Piaget, Maria
  Montessori, Jerome Bruner,
  "Marvin" comic strip compilations
Professional-quality baby scale—why
  wait for appointments with the
  pediatrician to see how much baby is
  gaining?

What Your Wife May Look Like

Throughout the final month your wife will generally give up on any effort to preserve her dignity. She will adopt the full-scale unapologetic waddle, go with minimalist hair care, and finally don the jungle-print muu-*moo* she swore she'd never wear. She alternates between wide-eyed hysteria and zombielike stupor, and takes off her shoes whenever she darn well pleases.

What to Take to the Hospital

Her bag is filled with extra socks, bed-clothes, a hairbrush, and everything else, but don't forget that you're probably going to be stuck in the hospital for a while yourself. Pack your bag now. Here are some recommendations:

- A pillow, for nodding off in chairs
- A pack of cards, for tossing into a hat from ten paces until your wife tells you to cut it out
- Toothbrush, comb, fresh shirt, but not a razor—the unshaven look is de rigueur for new papas
- Address book that includes phone numbers of all major relatives; or double check that cell phone is fully loaded with same
- A tennis ball, for giving excellent lower back massage, especially during back labor, and for bouncing mind-lessly off a wall until your wife tells you to cut it out
- A small harmonica. Did you know that you can teach yourself to play a few simple tunes in just minutes?
- A beeper. Not so people can reach you, but so the security guards will take you for a doctor and not make you sign in every time you pass through the lobby.
- A handful of quarters in case of prob-lems with the room phone. (Also good for tossing to see how close you

can land them to the wall until your wife tells you to cut it out.)

- This book. In those final hours, it's important to have a handy, reassuring reference work that includes everything you need to know about labor and delivery, so find one and take it along, too. This book, opened to about page 72–73, makes a handy eyeshade for catnaps.
- Food. She's chosen some nuts and dried fruit, but you need more than that to keep up your energy. Be sure to include the four basic food groups: fruits and vegetables (popcorn, ketchup, grape Kool-Aid); meats and fish (Slim Jims, pork rinds, Goldfish); cheese and dairy (Wheaties, Doritos, Tostitos, Pringles). Pop-Tarts also travel well, and fruit-filled Pop-Tarts encompass two essential food groups.
- Music. She'll ask for something soothing, but don't guess; ask about each choice *before* hitting play.
- Three stopwatches: one for timing contractions, one as an emergency backup, and one for timing how long you can hold your breath until your wife tells you to cut it out
- Pencil and pen, for recording important thoughts, instructions, and things to do, and for tossing up at the acoustic ceiling in an attempt to make them stick, until your wife says she'll throttle you with her bare hands, contraction or no contraction, if you come up with one more stupid stunt
- An expensive, beautiful, and incredibly thoughtful gift for your wife. Always a good idea during times of high stress.

WHAT YOU MAY BE CONCERNED ABOUT

The Due Date

"The doctors don't seem all that sure of the due date. Is there any simple way of judging how far along we are?"

In fact, there is. Much as timing contractions can tell you how far along labor has progressed, timing your wife's trips to the bathroom can give an excellent estimate of your due date. When she needs to urinate every hour, you can be sure labor is at least a month away. When visits occur every half-hour, she has about two weeks to go. Finally, when she is so completely exhausted from getting up constantly that she asks if you'd mind if she wet the bed, you can zip up the hospital bag and call work, because the long wait is nearly over.

By the way, don't tell her she can, because she just might, and you'll both regret it in the long run.

Crib Notes Childbirth Class

"I missed a lot of our birthing readiness classes. What do I absolutely need to know?"

Childbirth courses are much like high-school drivers' education courses. They're not strenuous, it's better to sit in the back, and the one thing not to miss is the films.

Preparation for childbirth—for the father—should be focused on one basic goal: not fainting at the sight of your newborn. The films of childbirth, though lacking in compelling dialogue, have a solid dramatic structure and will teach you one simple lesson: the greenish, slimy, blood-streaked thing hanging upside down in the doctor's hands is, in fact, a perfectly healthy baby. No matter how prepared you think you are, you will think that something is definitely terribly wrong. The films aren't pretty, but keep your eyes open, because the real thing is no prettier.

Aside from the films, of course, you'll want to learn a few breathing techniques and the information about all the available painkilling options so that you'll know how to explain to your wife why "you're not doing anything to help!" And don't get too riled up. You're something less than a nurse's assistant but more than an innocent bystander. The nurse and doctor will tell you what to do when the time comes.

The Baby

"As the big day approaches, my anxieties are driving me crazy. I've just got to know that our baby is going to be okay."

Try to relax. You've eaten right, avoided all the problems you could, done everything you could to improve your odds. And while we can't guarantee that your baby will be perfect, we can guarantee that your baby will be ugly. Yup. Ugly is a sure thing when it comes to newborns.

Sure, everyone will coo and say how beautiful the baby is, but most of them are seeing the kid after three or four days of recovery and respiration. You, however, will be face-to-face with this creature the very first moment that he or she looks around and says, "What the . . . !"

As is well known, newborns look like J. Edgar Hoover, Winston Churchill, or at best, the young Babe Ruth. However, the pudgy, wrinkled, droopy look is the least of it. Here are a few more reasons to keep photography to a minimum until a few days—or at least a few hours—have passed:

- The caput. An elegant name for a highly inelegant bump on the noggin.
- Sugar loaf molding. Another pretty name, but how pretty can elongation of the head possibly be? The passage through the birth canal essentially

squishes Baby's head into a point. As conehead Beldar might say, "We are from France, feel free to consume mass quantities."

- Boxer's nose. Says it all.
- Baby rug syndrome. In an apparent effort to hide their baldness, some babies are born with an all-natural bad toupee. This hair, often dark, long, and patchy, will fall out eventually and be replaced by new growth.
- Lanugo. Yes, it was a dance sensation from the late nineties, but it's also patches of downy hair that occur in the oddest places on newborns.
- Blotches. Call them angel kisses if it makes you feel better, but there is a whole assortment of potential birthmarks that will keep any baby off the box front of Ivory Snow.
- Milia. Or, yes, baby acne. Life is unfair, right from the start. At least most teenagers deserve what they get.
- Receding chin and silly-looking mouth. Don't worry, teeth will eventually give this area a lot more structure and dignity. Have you seen Gramps without his dentures?

Cold Feet

"I'm really concerned about keeping my cool during the delivery. I've never been too crazy about hospitals, and the sight of blood, IVs—I probably shouldn't go, right?"

Many men—indeed many people—feel uncomfortable in the hospital, and around the medical equipment and procedures involved in a modern birth. Perhaps you should consider home birth. Just kidding, but if we scared you, good. You can be thankful that you don't have any real responsibility in the hospital. It is time to man up! The least you can do is tag along and not faint at the sight of your wife's first blood test.

In many cultures, childbirth is the exclusive province of women. A mother, sister, or female friend is more likely to be present as the pregnant woman's companion. Too bad you don't live in one of those cultures. You will be mocked and ridiculed if you don't accompany your wife to the hospital. But if you are still concerned about being present, you two should talk it over. Share your feelings, your fears and discomfort. You'll still have to go, of course, but maybe she'll forgive you if you proceed to hit the floor at the sight of the epidural needle.

Chapter Eleven

Labor and Delivery

What Your Wife Will Be Complaining About

- Exhaustion

- You

- That willpower has no effect in making irregular contractions become regular

- You're timing contractions incorrectly

- That it's painful to walk; extremely painful to do anything else

- Pain

- Extreme pain

- That she can't decide when to go to the hospital

- Your attempt to start her on breathing techniques—it's too soon

- That there's no good reason to get total anesthesia

- That the nurse won't wait for the contraction to end before trying for the third time to hit a vein with the IV

- Medical science has made absolutely no progress on males giving birth

- Mr. Lamaze, whoever he was

- The hospital room

- That she can't believe her ob-gyn is not on call

- Her third-grade art teacher (logic has no meaning to a woman in labor)

- Peer pressure, which is keeping her from taking any and all available anesthetics

- It may not exactly be clear what she's complaining about, because it's hard to understand her through clenched teeth, but definitely not a happy face

- The doctors who don't seem to realize that no one has ever been in this much pain before

- Emotional highs and lows, fear, ecstasy, anxiety, and elation, often all at the same time

A Couple of Things to Say to Let Her Know You're Caring, Sensitive, and Up on the Required Reading

1. "You know, a prolonged active phase can be caused by a malposition of the baby. Could be a breech, the head hasn't descended into the pelvis, or there is cephalopelvic disproportion—and we all know how much that can hurt, right, honey?"

2. "Until the eighteenth century, women never lay down to give birth; they would walk or stand or squat—all of which are physiologically superior positions. It was the obstetrician to the French court, a doctor named Mauriceau, who introduced the practice of lying down—and the court's standards were widely imitated. I'm sorry, were you having a contraction?"

3. "You know, having the baby hurts, but apparently expelling the placenta afterward doesn't hurt a bit. That's something to be thankful for."

The POPGAR Test

With the increased involvement of fathers in the birthing process, with fathers even attending cesarean births, it became necessary to develop a hospital methodology for the fathers. The acronymic POPGAR test has become the norm. This simple test was developed in the late 1980s to help hospital personnel evaluate a father in those critical moments just after the birth of his child. He is rated on a scale of 0, 1, or 2 points, in six areas: Pallor, Optimism, Pride, Grimace, Activity, and Relatives. A total score of 7 or above indicates a healthy father; a low score may indicate a need for more careful observation.

How the POPGAR Test Is Scored

AREA	0	1	2
Pallor	White as a sheet	Washed out	Pale
Optimism	Thinks baby said "Dada"	Thinks baby is looking at him	Thinks baby is beautiful
Pride	Asks nurse if the paparazzi have been bothering her for details	Asks nurse if she's ever seen a more perfect baby	Asks nurse if all babies are so great
Grimace	Slack-jawed	Smiles hazily	Can't stop grinning
Activity	Nods off in a chair	Walks baby	Dances with baby
Relatives	Can't remember if he has relatives	He has called the key relatives	Has called all relatives and many complete strangers

Videotaping Your Delivery

Until hospitals lift their overly conservative policies restricting the delivery room to the woman and her partner or coach, there is only one way to share the experience of your labor and delivery with family and friends: the magic of digital video.

Nowadays the purchase of a video camera is as much a part of pregnancy as is painting the nursery. So don't wait until you bring the baby home to begin the documentary drama of life. And for goodness' sake, neither you nor your wife should be shy about taping these special hours for posterity. The camera may seem intrusive at times, and it's not always easy to think about your laboring wife's needs and keep an eye on the framing at the same time, but the laughs you'll share when you watch with relatives and co-workers will more than make up for any initial feelings of embarrassment.

How to make a quality tape? Thoughtfully, most modern hospital delivery rooms are extremely well lit. Amateur videographers are thus protected from that most common problem of low light. You will probably need a standard video light for the hospital room itself, but once active labor begins—at which time you may be distracted from your camerawork—the lighting is all taken care of. Some expectant fathers worry that they simply cannot function effectively as both cameraman and coach. Well, that's what tripods are for! Should your wife need a quick review of breathing techniques or someone to toss a stray curse at, you can be there—and still be getting it all down on tape. Unfortunately, the resulting video will be rather static, and you risk losing your audience's full attention. You may want to consider strapping a camcorder to a football helmet to create a perfectly serviceable "daddy-cam." A ten-dollar remote cable will allow you to operate the pause/record button with your teeth and still have both hands free for brow mopping and back rubbing.

When you're preparing to tape your child's birth, it is best to make everything as idiot-proof as possible, because with all the excitement and tension, it's easy to forget to charge the batteries or create in-camera graphics. Here are some simple videotaping tips for the delivery room:

- Don't ask the anesthesiologist to hold the microphone.
- Don't ad-lib a humorous voice-over as you shoot. You can add it later.
- Don't try to make the atmosphere seem "more personal" by asking the doctors and nurses to remove their masks.
- Never, ever tell your wife to push harder because you're running out of tape.

- Don't joke with the hospital personnel about the tape being good evidence for your upcoming malpractice suit.
- Don't video cesareans.
- Don't attempt to come up with similes to describe the moments-old newborn.
- Three hours is too long, even if you're planning to edit it down, and you'll never get around to editing it down, anyway.
- Please, please, please ignore all of the above and anything in this book, or in any book, that suggests you videotape your wife's delivery. First, most hospitals won't let you. Second, you don't want to do this, trust me. Third, sure there may be some things you'd like to remember in labor and delivery, but there is also a lot more you'll want to forget.

REAL ADVICE:

What You Never Expected When You're Expecting

Up to this point in this compendium of helpful guidance for expectant fathers, we have made every effort to give advice that is flippant, inconsequential, and for the most part extraneous, if not irrelevant. However, out of a sense of duty and moral responsibility, we felt it was important to delve into reality. What follows is genuine up-to-date information that will point you and your wife toward a wonderful, enriching childbirth experience. Through diligent research, we found these tidbits of reality—options in pregnancy, labor, and delivery for you to consider.

MALE CRAVINGS?

"We are for the first time asking men: Does becoming a father affect your hormones?" says Dr. Katherine Wynne-Edwards of Queen's University in Canada. "And the answer is: 'Yes, it does.'" The Canadian researcher tested men during the months when their wives were expecting and discovered increases in estrogen-like hormones, along with decreases in testosterone. These physiological changes were judged to be substantial enough to cause weight gain, morning sickness, and even food cravings.

INVITE FLIPPER

As reported in *USA Today* under the heading "Dolphin Births Nixed," a group of six British women were denied permission to deliver their babies in a special glass-walled water tank in the Red Sea. Their obstetrician hoped that being born among dolphins would give the infants a special affinity with nature and might improve human-dolphin communication. No specific reason was reported for the denial. I'd guess maybe it was that the applicants were judged to be nut bars.

INVITE THE NEIGHBORS

Unlike modern America, where laboring women are sequestered in hospitals, other societies have made birth a pleasant social affair. Family and friends—including children—gather to offer moral support for the young mother-to-be. Imagine all your nearest and dearest cheering you on through the entire labor and birth. It's good to be a repressed American.

TECHNOLOGY FROM NASA

Though the system is not particularly popular, some countries have allowed the use of a special decompression suit for the laboring mother. This suit lifts the abdomen away from the uterus during each contraction. The decrease in pressure on the uterus allows it to work more effectively, which means less pain for the mother.

ONLY IN SWEDEN

An innovation in natural childbirth has been pioneered in Sweden. Doctors there have found that using a Japanese-made cervical vibrator as often as three times during the first stage of labor allows the cervix to relax between contractions. This, in turn, allows the cervix to work more effectively with the contraction. Add your own joke here.

Fear of Switching

"I watch a lot of made-for-television movies. I guess what I'm trying to say is that I know it's probably ridiculous, but I'm terrified the hospital will somehow switch our baby."

No fear that you are feeling is ridiculous, but you should be reassured by the simple fact that only one in ten babies born in this country is accidentally switched with another at the hospital. Nonetheless, fear of a switch crosses the mind of almost every new parent. Did we say one in ten? We meant one in ten million births, and actually we just made up that figure, but it's probably some really big number like ten or twenty million. (Although, logically, it would have to be two in ten million, because if one gets switched, then there must be another one that got switched, too.)

That said, it is still worth putting your mind at ease by taking a few simple precautions as soon as your child is born. Sure, they have the coordinating mom-and-baby bracelets, but somehow that only adds to the sense of doubt. After all, the hospitals wouldn't have instituted the bracelet system if they weren't a little unsure of themselves, right? One father we know spent a few moments bonding with his newborn, and after deciding that he couldn't lock in on any particular distinguishing feature, he took a moment to put a discreet black X on his child's foot. Sure, the nurses were a little mystified, and his wife teased him relentlessly, but at least he came home with *his* baby. An indelible marker, a friendship bracelet, a quick haircut—whatever you do, don't rely on memorizing your baby's features. He may look unique at that first moment, but your perspective will be a little different when you're behind the glass of the hospital nursery looking at a whole roomful of squishy little faces.

Painkillers

"We're getting so much information about all the various options for pain relief— epidurals, analgesics, hypnosis—that it's dizzying. Aren't there any simple answers?"

Unfortunately, the process of labor and childbirth is a complicated matter, with many possibilities and probabilities to be considered. You may experience severe tension headaches, back strain, and even red, irritated eyes. When giving a back massage, you may find that your arms cramp up. When you nod off in a chair, your leg may fall asleep, which can lead a painful tingling when you try to use it. It can't be denied: Childbirth involves pain, for men.

Ideally, your childbirth preparation classes have taught you not to fear the pain. Though many of those one-sided classes tend to focus on women's issues, the same basic principles apply to you. Concentrate on your breathing. Use the pain; don't fight it so much as try to go with it. Most of all, relax as much as you can, whenever you can. If you can nod off between your wife's contractions, that's great.

Still, there may come a time for medical intervention and you shouldn't feel bullied into refusing it. Pay no attention to men who say that with medication you aren't "really experiencing" childbirth. These militant anti-medical-establishment types will tell you that a man's body was created with the ability to stand idly by while a woman is giving birth, without any help from doctors and medication. Make your own decision. If you decide you need a couple of aspirin for the headache, take them, by all means. (And bring your own, because the hospital won't give out any medication to nonpatients.) Feel free to do whatever you can to ease the pain during the long hours of labor and the intense pressure of childbirth. You deserve a little help in getting through it.

What to Say During Labor

"We took the classes, I've read the books, and I'm still not exactly sure what I'm supposed to say or do as labor coach, except that it has something to do with a tennis ball."

A. Many men go into labor—so to speak—terrified of saying the wrong thing and, in the midst of labor, are bored with saying the same thing over and over. And the tennis ball—suggested as a means of massaging the lower back—seldom actually comes into play. Neither does the giant blue yoga exercise ball that she made you carry into the hospital fully inflated.

What can you do? It's really not that complicated. First, you are your wife's willing slave, jumping at her every whim. Second, you are an interpreter between your wife and the hospital personnel, explaining to her what they are suggesting, and translating her grunts and snarls into relatively polite discourse. Third is the coaching part—and don't worry, the nurses handle the nitty-gritty. You didn't really think that you would be the one to make the call on when active labor has begun, or when to administer an epidural, did you? So don't worry about keeping an eye on the readouts from the fetal monitor. Plus, the nurses most likely know all the breathing gimmicks better than you do. So all you really have to do is provide encouragement and love. How? Stick to the basics, and if in doubt, remember that especially as labor progresses, less is more. Chitchat may only annoy her. Occasional eye contact may be all she wants. You're just a target for her glowering.

WHAT TO SAY TO YOUR WIFE DURING EARLY (FIRST-PHASE) LABOR

1. "Everything is packed and ready to go."
2. "I love you."
3. "I bought you a little present—just for being a wonderful person."
4. "I just have a feeling it's going to go smoothly."
5. Sing the complete lyrics to Paul Anka's "(You're) Having My Baby" while her sense of humor is still functioning. (Although strictly speaking, she should sing the second verse—which is an answer to the male voice of the first verse.)
6. "It must have been that Chinese food."
7. "I hope she looks like you."
8. "Just try to relax as much as you can."

WHAT *NOT* TO SAY TO YOUR WIFE DURING EARLY (FIRST-PHASE) LABOR

1. "Just relax as much as you can—labor can go on for days."
2. "This isn't another bogus false labor thing, is it?"
3. "I forget, which hospital is it again?"
4. "Either my stopwatch is broken or the contractions are slowing down."
5. "Can't we wait a little longer before we go to the hospital? It's the fourth quarter."
6. "Don't forget, this is the easy part."
7. "I just can't wait to have that baby."

WHAT TO SAY TO YOUR WIFE DURING ACTIVE (SECOND-PHASE) LABOR

1. "I love you."
2. "That's great."
3. "Good, beautiful."
4. "You're wonderful."
5. "Sure it does."
6. "You're doing great."
7. "Relax between contractions—that's it."
8. "You can do it."
9. "You're strong."
10. "Is there anything at all you want?"

WHAT *NOT* TO SAY TO YOUR WIFE DURING ACTIVE (SECOND-PHASE) LABOR

1. "You don't look like you're having fun." (Sarcasm might play during first-phase labor, but lose it for active labor.)
2. "You're not as relaxed as you should be." (Negativity.)
3. "I can't bear to see you in so much pain." (She needs strength, not pity.)
4. "I just figured out in my head how much this hospital is costing us per minute."
5. "You had the baby! Ha! Made you look."
6. "You think this is tough? Larry's wife was in labor for forty-three hours."
7. "Mind if I nap until the action starts?"

WHAT TO SAY TO YOUR WIFE DURING TRANSITIONAL (THIRD-PHASE) LABOR

1. "It's okay, you're okay."
2. "I love you."
3. "You're wonderful."
4. "You're working hard."
5. "You're doing great."
6. "Remember, just relax between contractions—don't anticipate the next one."
7. "We've waited a long time—and that baby's not that far away now."

WHAT *NOT* TO SAY TO YOUR WIFE DURING TRANSITIONAL (THIRD-PHASE) LABOR

1. "A friend of mine who's a doctor said that physiological evidence shows that labor ranks right up there with gunshot wounds on the pain scale."
2. "I've heard that there's a kind of amnesia so that women don't remember just how painful labor was."
3. "Do you think I look nice in the hospital regulation outfit?"
4. "Once I broke my wrist, and that sure hurt."
5. "I can't believe you haven't even broken your water yet."
6. "I've been having some second thoughts about the name we decided on."
7. "Don't blame me—it's nature."
8. "Do you ever wonder how competent all these doctors and technicians are?"

9. "Well, if you're not going to breathe with me, I'm just not going to bother breathing at all."

WHAT TO SAY TO YOUR WIFE DURING PUSHING, DELIVERY, AND AFTER

1. Nothing until after—she's not listening.
2. "You did it."
3. "You're wonderful."
4. "I love you."
5. "Look at our baby boy/girl."
6. "Thank you."

WHAT *NOT* TO SAY TO YOUR WIFE DURING PUSHING, DELIVERY, AND AFTER

1. "It's great that you're not worried about your modesty anymore."
2. "Look at what a mess this place is."
3. "You know what's another good name for a girl? Sylvia—isn't that a pretty name?"
4. "Eww—that's the baby?"
5. "Yes, I did it!"
6. "When can we have another one?"
7. "What a minute, that baby looks like Phil, our garage mechanic."
8. "How many days do you think you want to stay—two, three?"
9. "What should I do with all the dirty laundry at home?"

Taking Pictures

"Okay, you talked me out of videotaping our upcoming birth, but I'd like to take some photographs. Are there any problems with still photography in hospitals?"

Our advice is quite simple: Take your camera to the hospital but do not take any pictures until one full hour after the birth of your child. Any photographs of your wife in labor will not be appreciated; photographs of deliveries are best confined to pregnancy guides and medical textbooks; and newborns look a lot better once they've had a little breathing room. Also, go with high-speed film or set the digital on no flash so that you can minimize glare in your baby's eyes during the first hours of life. This is not for physiological reasons but for psychological ones. Taking too many photos can put the hour-old child at risk of contracting IPS (infant paparazzo syndrome)—a nonthreatening condition marked by an inflated sense of importance.

While we're on the subject, once you do begin taking hundreds and hundreds of digital photographs, please remember that while it is very easy to use Snapfish or Shutterfly to send everyone you know all 574 photos of Junior, and because they were in the same grouping, the seven shots you took of the leak above the kitchen you took for insurance purposes, it is not very considerate. Take that extra time to pick and choose. Thank you. From all of us.

Circumcision

"I always assumed that circumcision was done for medical reasons, but now I hear that it is no longer considered particularly beneficial."

Fathers who have attended their baby's circumcision are usually shocked to see what he has to go through. They often feel guilt and anguish over having authorized the procedure. This is a very good reason not to go and watch. Do you really want to see your newborn son placed in a "circumstraint" and see a hemostat applied, clamps, and . . . you don't even want to read about it.

Does it hurt? Are you kidding? It hurts just thinking about it. Some people tell themselves that the infant's nervous system is not fully developed. These people are fooling themselves. For certainly most little boy infants wail for all they're worth when the deed is done.

Is it worth doing? There is slim evidence of any medical advantages. The most common reason that 65 percent of American parents still choose circumcision is that 65 percent of American parents still choose circumcision. This fear of looking different may be unfortunate,

but it is not unreasonable. Looking different can be confusing for a young boy. The argument, based solely on aesthetics, that somehow it just looks better is a cover for the fact that 65 percent of baby boys start life with a little trim. And a few decades ago, that figure was 80 percent, so circumcision is generally on the decline. You may find that your medical team actively discourages it. If you'd like to get embroiled in impassioned debate about the virtue of an "intact" penis and the "mutilation" of our men-children, feel free to hop on the Internet, where there is sure to be a message board that will thoroughly tick you off, whichever side you take.

Of course, you may be Jewish. If you're not sure, don't worry about it. If you are, circumcision is more than just a little hospital procedure, it's a bris. This means you must wait the traditional eight days, and then have a mohel come remove in a special service what the forefathers had removed. (Or should it be foreless-fathers?) Relatives and friends gather in joyous celebration, complete with lox-and-bagel platters, while the little fellow and his mother are in the back bedroom sobbing. By the way, if you're Christian and feeling left out, you could celebrate the Circumcision (of Jesus, that is), which is January 1, although not many churches hold special services. And if they did, what exactly would they be praying for?

Rumors and speculation about circumcision's role in human sexuality are common but unfounded. It has never been proven that circumcised men can hold an erection longer, nor has it been proven that uncircumcised men experience greater sexual pleasure, although a government-funded group of researchers at Cornell University had a hell of a good time trying to find out.

Chapter Twelve

The First Weeks

What Your Wife Will Be Complaining About

- Exhaustion

- You

- Why does she still look pregnant if Baby is out?

- That she will never walk again—despite nurses' continued "you'll recover faster" urging her to try

- Perineal pain

- Fear of postpartum depression (technically known as prepostpartum depression)

- Fear of bowel movements

- Sore nipples if breastfeeding

- Fear of Tom Cruise stopping by to tell her there is no such thing as postpartum depression

- Whoever invented breastfeeding in the first place

- Your family's ill-timed visits, goofy gifts, and passive-aggressive comments

- The flowers—she doesn't want to leave any behind

- That the nurses are intrusive and patronizing

- That the nurses are never available and won't tell her anything

- That she did all the work; yet you seem to get half the credit

- That she initially felt that Baby was the most gorgeous cherub ever but the realization of baby's plug-ugliness is dawning

- Baby's belly button stump, which she finds really gross

- That Baby is already too big for the Philadelphia Eagles jumper you bought, although it's probably just as well

- The name you agreed on, which suddenly seems all wrong

- That Social Security already insists on giving your baby a number—it's creepy

- Emotional highs and lows, fear, ecstasy, anxiety, and elation, often all at the same time

A Couple of Things to Say to Let Her Know You're Caring, Sensitive, and Up on the Required Reading

1. "Hey look, I know what that is, that's meconium!"

2. "Sure, our baby looks a little yellow, but it's just mild jaundice. Thank goodness he doesn't have hemolytic jaundice from blood incompatibility—which could damage the nervous system."

3. "Watch—I can get the baby to do the Moro reflex, just by dropping her."

4. "Did you know that the discovery of the hand—a baby noticing its own hand—is one of the essential steps toward psychomotor coordination?"

What Did You Expect?

It may come as a shock, but when you get home from the hospital, you'll quickly realize that being pregnant was the easy part. Especially for you, the expectant father. Oh sure, there were a lot of inconveniences, minor aches and pains, nettlesome planning, and some baby furniture to assemble, but none of it can compare to the early days of fatherhood.

Pregnancy is neat and contained; fatherhood is all over the place. The baby's in the bassinet, the bottles are boiling, the baby needs a change, your wife would love a cup of tea, the baby needs a change, the two A.M. feeding, the four A.M. feeding, the desperate five A.M. drive around the block, the baby needs a change and in the middle of it puts on a stunning free-form aerial demonstration and now both the baby

and you need a change, "Good morning, we're out of coffee," how could the baby need a change I just changed the baby, time to make the doughnuts. And off to work with you, with only a little "cottage cheese" on your shoulder.

You suddenly feel nostalgic for morning sickness. Remember when days would go by without much more than an "Oh, feel here, honey, she's kicking!" or an awkward attempt to give a back rub to someone who is all front? And when you went to sleep you could sleep until morning. Didn't even seem that special, sleeping till morning. You know, just close your eyes, drift off, and wake up in the morning. "Good night, see you in the morning." Just one night! Just one night straight through! Is that so much to ask?

Relax. Sleep deprivation, with its attendant psychoses and hallucinations, is a perfectly natural part of early parenting. Many experts on early childhood and parenting agree that only by this "disassociation from reality" can the parent survive the trauma of the first six months.

Crying

Q.

"Crying at night, crying first thing in the morning, I can't take it anymore—and the baby cries a lot, too. And what should I do when the baby and wife are both crying? Who should I go to first?"

A.

You might think that babies cry all the time, and that a crying adult would always be first priority, but think again. If you go to your wife to console her, the howling of the baby will only make you both so tense and anxious that you'll end up snapping, "Quit blubbering" and she'll say, "You don't deserve a family because you don't care about anyone but yourself," and the baby will still be screaming like a banshee with a hotfoot, and she'll say, "Just go away, you make me sick," and you'll say, "Nothing would make me happier than to leave you and your misery," and then you'll go get the baby finally, and your wife will still be crying or possibly calling her mother, or even a lawyer, and it turns out that the baby had her arm stuck in the side of the crib and now you feel really bad, the baby hates you, the wife hates you, and you've got to get up in the morning and head into a corporate headquarters where there are at least a handful of people who also hate you, or at best are angling for your job. So if you're still concerned about crying, yes, it's okay to cry. As long as no one sees you.

Taking Care of Mom

Q.

"I run my own business and can't afford to stay home from work for too long, but I want to take good care of my wife, too."

A.

More and more men are able to be at home during these first weeks, thanks to paternity leave in specific and male enlightenment in general, but for some it won't be possible. If your wife buys your particular excuse, you're past the biggest hurdle, but you'll still want to arrange some kind of help for her.

The first option is, of course, her mom. You probably don't have much choice in this matter. If they've worked it out, Mom will be waiting on the doorstep when you bring the baby home. And if you've never appreciated your mother-in-law, you will now. An extra nap and a warm meal never looked so good. You'll probably forgive her for everything. Of course, when the baby is learning to walk, it might be time to suggest politely that she is pushing the limits of her welcome.

Another option is your mom. Just kidding.

Finally, if you can afford the luxury, look for a doula service. It's a Greek term meaning "to mother the mother," which seems like a lot of idea for two syllables, but then those Greeks have a very impressive-looking alphabet. The people who provide this service are usually RNs or LPNs, but in addition to taking care of the baby and instructing the new mom, they are a sympathetic companion for her, and do light housekeeping, even cooking and laundry. It's pricey but if you can't be there yourself, assuage your guilt and fork over the moola for the doula.

Hair Loss

"Maybe I'm imagining it, but I think I'm losing hair more rapidly."

There is still disagreement in the medical community over this issue. Pregnancy—and postpartum in particular—is a traumatic period for the father, both emotionally and physically. Could this cause hair loss and accelerated balding?

Women in the postpartum period will also suffer hair loss, but this is definitely a temporary physiological experience. High hormone levels during pregnancy cause hairs that would ordinarily fall out to stay. Her hair will get thicker throughout the nine months but, with childbirth, decreases in those hormone levels will cause the extra hair to fall out. This is a natural process that may be shocking, but it does not lead to baldness.

In men, the news is not so cheery. Hair loss is hair loss, like it or not. Could trauma be at the root of the problem? Most scientists believe that balding is solely determined by genetics, others believe that physical and emotional factors have an effect, and a small minority believe that tiny hair elves come and pluck at the scalps of men who have been bad.

There is hope. The national epidemic of balding is beginning to get the public attention and scientific funding it deserves. Many old theories of balding are now being tested in research labs. The it's-determined-by-your-mother's-father's-hair genetic theory has been disproved by the author; our forehead is ever heightening, while Grandfather sports his dignified shock of white hair at seventy-seven years. The promulgators of such theories should think twice about the false confidence they inspire—and about our broken hearts, for cripes' sake.

Other theories have also been put to rest. Does hat-wearing cause baldness? Definitely not, although researchers have established that balding does cause hat-wearing. Conspiracy theorists who believe that the International Hair Club for Men has put something into the nation's water supply have yet to produce hard evidence.

Our advice is not to worry too much. You'll still have more hair than the baby, for a few months anyway.

Going Back to Work

"We keep having the whole working versus stay-at-home debate—Can we afford daycare? What are the best options? Will spending all day with nothing but kids be mind-numbing? Will time away be a major career setback? Will we feel like the kids are being raised by a nanny? It all comes down to one question: Should I go back to work?"

Yes. You have to.

Fear of Changing

"I don't like changing diapers. Can we start toilet training now that the baby is a week old?"

No, you may not, you sniveling wimp. You're so far away from toilet training, it's funny. But the most-feared task in fathering is also the most overrated. Changing diapers is no big deal. In the first two years of life, you will become completely inured to many grosser

tasks. If you want something to feed your nightmares, try these:

- Taking the baby's temperature with the rectal thermometer
- Sucking snot out of the baby's nose with a nasal aspirator
- We don't even want to talk about it—but it has to do with constipation
- Catching vomit in your hand, because you didn't have a spit-up diaper handy
- Blowing baby's nose with your bare hand, using either a discreet fling or a sock for disposal
- Using your own former toothbrush to clean a wicker chair that met up with a leaky diaper

It would be needlessly alarmist to go into great detail about the potential disasters that loom, but we must give one simple warning: Never play "flying baby" while lying on your back with your mouth open right after the baby has been fed.

The Name

"I can't get used to the name we gave this baby. It just doesn't seem to be sticking. Is it possible we picked the wrong name?"

Many new parents can't get used to the idea that they can just give this new creature a name. Assigning a name, after all, is a quintessential expression of power. Adam—the first man—was given the task of naming all the other creatures.

If you knew your baby's gender and picked a name months ago, it may seem more natural to you. It is simply a matter of finally making a formal introduction. But if you're one of those who waited, laying a name on this baby may seem impossible. What if Baby doesn't like it?

Have you really chosen the wrong name? Impossible! You considered, you debated, you settled on the name you both thought was right. Stick with it. (Actually, it is statistically possible—about one in twenty thousand—that you have chosen a name so bad that it actually is wrong, like Phlegma or Tohmas. In these cases, the courts are very lenient and allow name changes with a minimum of legal entanglements.) The name you have chosen is the right one, but getting used to it can still be difficult. A silly nickname is often the answer. By calling your infant Fluffernutter or Baldy for a while, you can adjust yourself to the idea that the little ball of pudge is Cynthia, Gilbert, or Ariadne. And if you never really do get used to the name, the worst thing that can happen is that you'll end up with a twenty-five-year-old son in medical school who still goes by the name Wizzer.

Wisdom of the Fathers

"Now that the baby is here and happy and healthy, I've got a whole new set of anxieties. Number one is: Who am I to teach this little bundle of joy all about the meaning of life?"

You've learned to be a decent friend: concerned, engaging, sympathetic. You've started learning to be a decent spouse: sharing, loving, supportive. But a father has to be all that and also *wise*. Whether you have any wisdom to offer or not, someday your child will ask—expecting reasonably complete, comprehensible answers—whether dogs go to heaven, why there is war, why some people are poor, why Aunt Susan never got married, why are they allowed to sell cigarettes if they're bad for you, why it isn't stealing when you take envelopes and paper from the office. And you thought why is the sky blue and what are belly buttons for were tough!

How can you prepare for the interrogations? There are a few simple plans. Misdirection can work: "Wanna see a neat magic trick?" Deflection is fairly reliable: "Ask your mother." But ultimately, you're going to have to bite the bullet and accept responsibility for the fact that you have led a fairly unexamined life. Perhaps now would be a good time to get in touch with your spiritual side, wrestle with some ethical issues, and decide what your purpose on Earth is. You'll need something to ponder while you're walking back-and-forth with a squalling baby on your shoulder.

In a related matter, in case you're worried about "the talk," here's one simple approach. Go full bore with the antiquated birds-and-bees, pollen-and-stamens metaphor explanation. Not to save yourself embarrassment, mind you, but you would hate to spoil the surprise of the sixth-grade health class films, right?

Finally, if you're really concerned from a philosophical perspective about the influence you will have on your children, just read up on the latest, rather counterintuitive sociological research that shows that ultimately parents are one of the least influential factors in raising good kids. You rank well behind "peers" and just slightly ahead of "astrological sign." So, rest easy; even the wisest counsel will go in one ear and out the other.

The Balloons

Q. *"Aren't balloons a major hazard for kids? What am I supposed to do with all these 'It's a Boy' balloons?"*

A. Over the coming years, you'll be told by intrusive strangers that you are irresponsible and a bad parent for such crimes as letting your kids play with balloons or have popcorn, flinging them in the

air, or not brushing their hair out of their eyes. The best response is always to act as though they have single-handedly saved your child's life and reformed you as a parent forever. That seems to be what they are expecting.

The potential danger of balloons is that a popped balloon can be swallowed or inhaled, and the rubber is particularly hard for doctors to locate. However, you will also find that kids love balloons. Denied, balloons may become an obsession. All the more reason that Mylar "It's a Boy/Girl" helium balloons have completely replaced traditional rubber balloons. Better still, these extraordinary inventions last up to five hundred times longer. In fact, some of these Mylar balloons have become family heirlooms, passed on, still aloft, from generation to generation.

Child Care

Q. *"Life is so complicated with the new baby here, I haven't had time to begin looking for a live-in nanny. And, of course, we're concerned about making a good choice."*

A. Ah, yes. Trouble finding just the right fully qualified and trustworthy candidate for the full-time child care position? What do you want? Sympathy? Why don't you have the butler make a few phone calls for you, set up some interviews with your personal secretary, and once they've got it down to two or three candidates, you can set down your drink by the pool and come inside long enough to pick one. That shouldn't be too much of a strain.

Actually, perhaps we're not being entirely fair. Today more and more women with middle-class incomes find that they must go back to work so that they can afford to pay for full-time child care. All right, that's still not fair because many women do need to work for economic reasons, and any woman certainly has the right to combine work and motherhood.

The choice between being a working mother and working as a mother is a difficult one, and the two camps are breaking out into what has become a national "Mommy War." Women on both sides try to keep an open mind but simply have no idea how the other side could possibly have made such a limiting, impractical, and essentially wrong decision. What is the husband's role? We'll give you a clue. It is *not* to carefully consider and weigh the pluses and minuses of each position. All right, we'll give you another clue. *Don't* even come close to forming an opinion until your wife has made up her mind, then totally agree with her. There's a war going on out there, and loose lips sink ships.

Chapter Thirteen

Life with Baby

What Your Wife Will Be Complaining About

- Exhaustion

- You

- That Baby smiled at her but everyone insists that it's just gas

- Sleep deprivation

- Breastfeeding—though easier now, it's still not exactly fun

- Breast pump

- Spit-up

- Diapers

- Fears of inadequacy as a mother

- Hospital bills, paperwork

- Inadequacy of local public schools

- The injustice of it all

- After all those years of *Conan* being on too late, now it's over too early

- The high cost of college education

- That clipping a baby's fingernails is terrifying

- That Baby's beautiful blue eyes are quickly fading to brown

- Ridiculously high-pressure and totally unnecessary educational programs (French for Tots, Math Readiness, Baby Swimmers, etc.)

- Expense of same

- Birthmark that "would fade" but hasn't

- That the doctor gave the baby an "outie"

- Black-and-white high-contrast educational toys—they're ugly

- Too many stuffed animals already

- Prolonged exposure to babies is making adult parts of her brain atrophy

- Designated-hitter rule (okay, but wouldn't it be cool if she did?)

- Emotional highs and lows, fear, ecstasy, anxiety, and elation, often all at the same time

A Couple of Things to Say to Let Her Know You're Caring, Sensitive, and Up on the Required Reading

Remember, these suggestions are based on actual scientific studies.

1. "You know, another good reason that breastfeeding is preferable to the bottle is that breast milk has twice as much taurine, a nonprotein nitrogen compound, as there is in cow's milk (which is what most formulas are composed of). Taurine seems to be a necessary neurotransmitter or neuromodulator, and not only do babies have a limited enzymatic capacity for synthesizing taurine from precursors, but premature infants have been shown to have high concentrations of taurine in their blood, and I don't have to tell you what that means. Do I? And by the way, taurine is the same ingredient that Red Bull touts on the can, so really what they're selling is breast milk with caffeine."

2. "Projectile vomiting—that is, vomiting that travels some distance away from the baby—though a bit terrifying, isn't a sure sign of a problem unless it happens frequently, once or twice every day."

3. "While constipation is a common problem in babies, it is very treatable, with the very rare exception of Hirschsprung's disease, a total constipation caused by malfunctioning intestinal muscles. I wonder if Mrs. Hirschsprung thought it was a good idea to give it the family name?"

What to Buy During the First Year

Just because you've been spending money all pregnancy long doesn't mean you can quit now. There's so much more your child needs, today!

ESTIMATED COSTS, THE FIRST YEAR
Basics: $1,235
  (Does not include either diaper service at $90 per month or disposables at $125 per month)

Basics plus extras: $6,285

Basics
Baby sunglasses
French for Tots
Gymboree classes
Home hair-cutting kit
Infant CPR classes, for you
Music time
Name in hand-tooled wood blocks

Professional portrait photos
Shoelace clamps (keeps 'em tied)
Spill-proof Cheerio/raisin dispenser
Toddler leash
Wee Playhouse acting workshops

Extras

Baby's own business cards
Baby's own home computer
Dog for Baby
Horseback riding lessons
Nicer pajamas/bathrobe—since you're
   wearing them out of the house when
   going for sleep-inducing drives
Tree house
Subscribe to VCAST phone videos
   (they market them as a way to
   see music videos; but they are
   mostly used to download *Blue's
   Clues* snippets to use as emergency
   distractions)

Total Childproofing

Making your home or apartment safe
for your child isn't as complicated as you
may believe. Yes, there are childproofing services that will survey your home
and make recommendations and instal-
lations, but nothing they do takes more
than a little research, a bit of common
sense, and the most basic carpentry. Sure,
there are whole catalogs full of childproofing equipment, but you only need
to buy what your home requires. How
much does your home require? Where

should you draw the line on childproofing? The final decision is your own.

There are certain basics that should
be considered essential—outlet plugs,
doorway gates, locks for the kitchen
cabinets—beyond these items, each
couple needs to find a level of comfort.
If additional gates and baby monitors in
every room make you feel secure, and
thus help you relax, then they've accom-
plished something before your baby
even comes home from the hospital.

If you know you want total childproofing, you can call in consultants—
they're in your local Yellow Pages—or do
it yourself with the following products.

The Kitchen: Where Disaster Lurks

DISHWASHER "DUMMY" CONTROL PANEL: Because these controls are by far the most
fascinating to the toddler, it may be
worth installing a false front with knobs
and levers they can adjust at will.

FLOOR STUBBIES: Small rubber knobs glued
onto the floor add traction to otherwise
slick linoleum.

COMBINATION LOCK KNIFE BLOCK: A simple
four-number code allows you to remove
knives.

CHILDPROOF DOG/CAT FOOD DISH: Miracle
electronic sensory device prevents your
child from tasting Spot's dinner but

allows the pooch to eat at will. (Warning: will not function properly if your child has whiskers.)

The Bathroom

CHILDPROOF TOILET LID: Safe for kids and lots of fun at parties, when guests can't figure out the "simple" four-step unlocking mechanism.

GENTLE FLUSH SYSTEM: Patented commode soundproofing cushions and minimizes the loud and potentially frightening sound of the toilet flushing. Why should toilet training be any scarier than it already is? Gentle Flush II plays dramatic classical themes to accompany toilet-based activities.

MEDICINE CABINET LOCK 'N' STOR: Medicines are simply too dangerous to keep in the home. This national chain of warehouses will rent you a small medicine cabinet far across town, five or six flights up, and double locked so that you and a Lock 'n' Stor employee must both be present with keys to open it.

TOILET PAPER SENSOR: Alarm sounds when more than five feet of toilet paper is unrolled all at once.

THE DOLLOPATOR: Automatically dispenses a single dollop of training toothpaste, and no more, until reset by an adult.

Because even these new toddler-safe training toothpastes are not, after all, a dessert topping.

All Around the House

VCR LOCK: Prevents small fingers from reaching in, from putting small items or food inside the machine, and from recording episodes of *Dora the Explorer* over your tapes of the 2000 World Series.

BICYCLE HELMETS: Not just for cycling anymore! How many bumps on the noggin will your children suffer before you realize that this light, impact-absorbing shell with Velcro chin fastener should be the first thing they put on in the morning?

CHOKE TESTER TUBE: New and improved version no longer includes removable lid that proved to be a hazard for children three and under.

SPRAYCOAT (PATENT PENDING): A simple one-step answer to all your childproofing needs. SprayCoat technicians cover every inch of your home with a soft, thick but transparent polymer. There'll be no hard edges anywhere, cleanups are a breeze, and you can stop feeling guilty about all the unread books on your shelves because they're permanently sealed in place.

WALL SWITCH GUARD: Not strictly a safety item, but it will prevent kids from discovering how much "fun" it is to flick lights on and off incessantly.

INDUSTRIAL METAL LATHE SAFETY GUARDS: Don't you hate it when you have to shut down your high-speed industrial lathe, just because Junior has toddled into the den? Not a problem with our six-step system that includes a child-size welder's mask, a flameproof baby jumper tested at six hundred degrees, and "Don't Touch the Rotating Metal Rod" signs.

ELECTRICAL CORD CAMOUFLAGE: You've tried taping them down, buying covers, even living without electricity. Now try decorating those troublesome electrical cords with our trompe l'oeil paint kit to make them blend into wood floors, carpets, even the most intricate oriental rugs.

Alarms

NATURAL GAS DETECTOR: Why let your home turn into a massive ticking time bomb? Will also pick up radon, carbon monoxide, methane, and problem halitosis.

POOL ALARM: When the pool water is disturbed, the alarm goes off. Great for knowing when it has started raining, or when wind is blowing.

TV RADIATION MONITOR: Measures levels to help minimize the damage of television radiation. (Plus, we've found that when sitting forty feet from the set, kids tend to lose interest.)

GPS JR!: If you can get your kids used to wearing a global positioning tracking collar when they're little, maybe when they're teenagers, you'll know where they are.

What to Read
WARNING: SHORT DIATRIBE AHEAD!

Would you like your kid to be smart? Sure, you would, and there is absolutely no mystery about how to accomplish that. The less TV they watch and the more books you read to them, the smarter they will be. There will come a time for TV but, before they can demand it, why give it to them? As soon as they will sit still in your lap, start reading them books. Read and read and read some more. In the short term, they'll learn language, to interpret ideas, and to follow logical patterns. In the long term, they'll be smart and successful and won't live in your basement until they are twenty-eight. Okay, lecture over.

Life is busy. The TV gives you a much-needed break. Every time you sit down to read a few good-night stories, you fall asleep before your kid does. That is a legitimate problem. Let's face it; even the best books for toddlers are pretty boring. (You don't see too many guys on the commuter train with their heads buried in *Goodnight Moon.*) There is a lot of discussion of colors and letters, cows and doggies; plenty of bold, simple colors; and not much drama. To make reading as painless as possible, try to find books that you can stand—and don't give in to your child's demand to read the same book over and over. Sure, they would enjoy it, but you've got to maintain your sanity. If you're truly dedicated, you can make trips to the library a regular part of your schedule. If not, you'll need a shelf of books that can stand up to repeated readings. There are plenty of reviews and advisors available out there. Here are just a few warnings, pitfalls, and gems.

The Tale of Peter Rabbit by Beatrix Potter is a classic, charming, oh-so-British morality tale with beautiful illustrations by the author. A few of her other books—*The Tale of Two Bad Mice* and *Tom Kitten*—are also pleasant diversions, but do not be fooled into thinking that the twenty-three-volume complete works is a good purchase. First off, many of the stories feature main characters that are trying to eat one other. Second, the syntax is hard to parse and the storytelling is just plain odd. And if you're confused, surely your two-year-old will be, too.

On the other hand, you can hardly go wrong with Dr. Seuss. A handful of the later books—*The Lorax* and *Oh The Places You'll Go*—get a bit pedantic and moralistic, but everything else is a joy from cover to cover. The carefully constructed metrical rhythms put almost every other children's "poet" to shame. The more you delve in the lazy rhymes and awkward scansion in other writers, the more you'll appreciate the good Doctor.

While we're near the "I Can Read It Myself" books in the Random House collection, do not overlook the works of P. D. Eastman, especially *Go, Dog. Go!* This may look at first glance like exactly the wrong sort of book to read over and over. There are only about fifty discrete words. There is only the loosest of story lines, and every page is just more dogs, dogs at play, dogs at work, dogs going around . . . "Go around again!" And yet, through some miracle, it is in fact one the most rereadable short texts ever created. Personally, I compare the prose style to early Hemingway. "The sun is up. The sun is yellow. The yellow sun is over the house." *A Farewell to Arms?* Nope. *Go, Dog. Go!*

When you spend enough hours poring over the great works of children's literature, you're bound to make some interesting discoveries. They say the mark of a classic is that you can always find something new in it. For example, in *Madeline*, when the lead is off in the hospital having her appendix removed, and after the eleven remaining girls have paid their visit and returned home in "two straight lines," there are still *twelve* little girls in the illustration "who break their bread" at dinner! A small continuity error that has been in print since 1939. It is also fun to find the little choices that authors made in earlier eras that today's editors and school librarians would no doubt squelch. When *Curious George* comes on board the ship in his very first adventure, the man in the yellow hat lets him smoke a pipe after dinner. Just another good reason to read—all the odd things you'll find yourself explaining to a two-year-old.

What to Expect in Your Mailbox

If you think that J. Crew and Pottery Barn catalogs are putting wear and tear on your mailbox, just wait for the postpartum postal deluge. As soon as America's legal conspiracy—mail order marketing lists—registers that you have been blessed with a bouncing baby consumer, the catalogs will come. Why is it that e-mail spam filters took only a few years to be pretty darn effective, while we've been suffering with junk mail for a half-century?

On the other hand, the marketers do it because it works. They know you will buy. Even more than chamois shirts and humorous boxer shorts, even more than Victoria's Secret (what exactly is she keeping as a secret? I've looked through the catalog again and again, and I still don't know), and even more than sharpening our image, we as a nation are willing to spend money on our kids. Recession or depression, our instinct to provide takes over. Even as we drive that nine-year-old Toyota into the ground, clip coupons, tuck Tupperware into the briefcase, and take vacations in the backyard, we are still willing to recite our magic number (and expiration date) to an operator so that the kids can each have "a wooden puzzle of their own first name."

Or an adorable lavender-and-mint jumpsuit from Hanna Andersson. Or a couple of pairs of those Sara's Prints pajamas—the ones that aren't actually called pajamas because the government won't allow plain cotton items to be sold as sleepwear because they're not fire retardant, but you know and we know that they *are* pajamas. While we're getting 100 percent cotton, let's get a couple of those organic cotton one-pieces for infants from the Natural Baby catalog and a few sweatshirts from Playclothes (and where can you get baby "work clothes")—or maybe the sweatshirts in After the Stork are better, or cheaper? We'll take both. Say, is that a Disney catalog? Hit me with a couple of movies, and the Donald Duck slippers, don't babies need slippers? A catalog from Back to Basics classic toys?—we'll take whatever we used to have—fun or not.

Are we spoiling this baby? Let's see what we can get that'll really be good for them. Aha, we'll take the metric number rods from Early Learning Center, the marble run from Sensational Beginnings, the big block set, no not that one, the really big one from Constructive Playthings, something from the Right Start—whatever, it just sounds like a good place to order—send us two of your finest dress-up outfits and throw in some face paints. Hearthsong? Some finger paints or finger puppets or both—do you have any paint-puppets? That should do it for now. Oh, wait! Oriental Trading Company! The official home of party-favor toys and themed junk, and the best place to shop when you're buying a gross of something.

Oh, never mind, let's go online . . . searching for "Rock 'em Sock 'em Robots" . . . not the new one, the one I had in 1979—omigosh, a complete vintage set of Wacky Packages stickers! Just what Baby needs!

WHAT YOU MAY BE CONCERNED ABOUT

Going Back to Work

"Can I go back to work yet?"

Ah, yes, work. The halcyon place where coffee breaks are not broken dreams—they actually happen. A place where screaming, wailing, sobbing, and moan-

ing are reserved for those infrequent discussions of salary. Most important of all, a place where each individual is responsible for his or her own bathroom needs. It's a place full of grown-ups, peace, and quiet.

And no, you can't go back to work. You've got time off, mister. You've come a long way, baby. Paternity leave is more and more common, thanks to more flexible work schedules, more progressive corporate attitudes, and management's realization that a man who isn't sleeping through the night is a liability anyway. When it all seems to be too much, remember that before long—a few weeks, at most a few months—you'll be back in the rat race, the lovely, predictable, satisfying nine-to-five. Your wife can take care of the home front. Or best of all, you can both go back to work and hire someone to raise your children. Remember, never *ever* say, even jokingly, that you'd love to stay home and be the primary caretaker. Sure, it'll make you sound hip, but you may later have the words *verbal contract* flung in your face.

Safety Can Be Fun

"We've childproofed every last corner of our home, but when I look at some of the toys we've got, frankly, I get scared. How can we know what's safe?"

After childproofing your home, it would

be foolish to outfit your child with toys that are death traps—things like balloons (choking hazard) and wooden blocks (sharp edges, weight); so be sure to use common sense in choosing playthings. It's not easy to find toys that are truly, thoroughly safe, but here are four basic items that we especially recommend for the safety-conscious parent:

NO-GO BIKE: Looks just like the real thing, but your kids can push the pedals all day long without risky movement.

SPONGE BLOCKS: Old-fashioned wooden blocks are too hard, and these stack almost as well and double as cleaning accessories for those major spills.

TEDDY BORE: What's the danger in traditional stuffed animals? Kids can get too attached to their favorite, dragging it everywhere and drooling on it, among other things, and this can create a sanitary disaster area of a toy. The Teddy Bore is specially designed and thoroughly tested; he will not have any lasting appeal to most children. His humorless expression, scratchy surface, and faint mildewy odor guarantee it.

CRAYON-ISH NONMARKERS: Sixty-four fabulous colors, neatly sorted and labeled, able to be dumped out, sorted, broken, peeled, tasted, and dumped out again—but completely unable to make a mark! That's right, these inert plastic cylinders won't mark walls, floors, or activity books!

Flying Babies

"We really want to take our baby to my parents for Christmas, but that means a long airplane flight. When will the baby be ready to fly? And what can we do to prepare?"

The one great thing about flying with an infant is that, for once, your appearance with Baby in your arms will *not* be greeted with oohs and aahs of admiration. As you walk down the aisle, all eyes will be upon you, but the looks will communicate thinly veiled dread that your seat will be nearby. It's a pleasant change.

Actually, traveling with an infant is much easier than traveling with babies a year or older, up to about fourteen years of age. By that age, traveling becomes easy again because your child will simply remain sullen and quiet, hoping to achieve the effect that they are, in fact, traveling alone. Up until that age, anything can happen. An infant may be lulled to sleep by the plane's vibration and the white noise of the engines. Or the baby will scream bloody murder from start to finish.

If babies had been meant to fly, they would have been born with more fully developed inner ear systems. As it is, uncomfortable air pressure during descent and ascent affects them more than it does adults. Prepare a bottle and have it ready, as swallowing can alleviate the discomfort. Another handy tip: Teach your two-month-old infant how to chew gum, which will ease the air pressure, help with teething, and give a charming "wizened street urchin" look.

The Farmer in the Dell

Call me selfish, but I think I'll lose my mind if I have to drive around listening to vapid children's music compilations of 'Head, Shoulders, Knees, and Toes,' or 'Whistle While You Work.'"

Have no fear! While there are still frightening CD collections of Barney, Raffi, Disney, and those generic "various" artists all singing the same grating kid songs ("Here We Go Loopty Loo," "Frère Jacques," and "This Old Man" in particular have the ability to freeze the soul), more and more legitimately cool artists have seen the need for kids' music that parents can stand. Look for They Might Be Giants, Tom Chapin, Dan Zanes, and Buckwheat Zydeco.

Of course, the problem is that little kids don't particularly like these albums. When they get old enough to compromise, try classic *Sesame Street* albums and the Backyardigans. Or just play the Beatles and think of it as an important part of their education.

Superman Syndrome

"We've heard all about the modern-day 'superwoman' juggling career and motherhood, but what about us? Am I wrong in feeling that I've fallen into a Superman syndrome—trying to do it all?"

We may be going out on a limb, but it's fair to say that trying to balance family and career can be just as difficult for a man as for a woman. Maybe *more* difficult. Yeah, more difficult, that's it. The pressures and expectations are just too much—we have no role models. Our own fathers were absent or misinformed, and probably both. Today's father drives himself crazy trying to be the perfect supportive and dedicated husband, the merciless career juggernaut at work, and still a loyal pal to the boys in the poker circle.

It's up at four A.M. on Saturdays to go trout fishing, back to the house by nine to make waffles, then you've got to get the groceries and do the laundry in time to sit back and enjoy the afternoon's ball game. A quick jog so you don't go completely to pot, whip up a stew for dinner, do the dishes, repair that kitchen drawer that keeps falling out, repaint the bathroom, and then run out and rent a movie to watch together that evening. It's one thing after another, and altogether too exhausting.

When the baby comes, you will simply have to make choices. No man can be a scratch golfer and bake from scratch, too. And golfing is more fun than baking. So, relax. You'll just have to settle for second best now and then. You can't "do it all," so don't try. Be ready to compromise now and then. If you need to stay late at the office, stay; she'll understand. If you need to take the boys from the office out to a great batting cage, she'll understand. But cut a few corners at work, too. Try making a short phone call to your wife from work, just to see how she's doing—the few minutes you lose won't cost you that promotion—and it would mean a lot to her. There are plenty of ways to show her you care. You could cash in your chips and have the poker game in time to get home for the two A.M. feeding, just for one example.

Little things like that mean a lot to a new mother. And if all the pressures just seem to be too much, hit the panic button and escape. Think: When was the last time you did something just for you? Take a weekend off from the home front and play thirty-six holes of golf. The more relaxed and happy you are, the better a helpmate you'll be when you *are* around. Right?

Oh well, they seemed like good ideas to us.

Postpartum Medical School Syndrome

"My wife just had a baby and now she has decided she wants to go to medical school and become a doctor. She seems quite serious about this. Will it wear off?"

It may seem strange, but the PMS^2 trend is becoming more and more common. Postpartum medical school syndrome occurs in varying degrees in one out of four new mothers. For some, it is only a bothersome regret that they didn't pay more attention in tenth-grade biology. For others, it leads to years of training and an MD.

Why does it happen? Well, a little knowledge is a dangerous thing. Your wife has done nine months of intensive reading in pregnancy books, which present detailed medical information and are also full of criticism of the male hegemony in the medical profession, which is blamed for everything from the high rate of cesareans to the parking problems around the hospital.

After all this research into medical possibilities, options in anesthesia, hospital regulations, and obstetrical innovations, your wife—no matter what her career up to this point—will feel that she missed her true calling and that she must become a doctor. So you are not alone, and it is certainly foolish to oppose your wife's wishes. Why try to stop her when the complexities of first-year biochemistry will probably do the job, without all the emotional underpinnings, the failure to be supportive, and all that?

And if she does become a doctor, look on the bright side: Now you can play golf together.

Success

"I don't want to push my kid, but I do want to make sure that he's stimulated and enriched and . . . all right, I do want to push my kid, okay?"

Everybody wants their baby to grow up happy and generous, socially graceful and successful, well-educated, with a profession, impressive titles, advanced degrees, loads of money, world travel, a wonderful spouse, and perfect grandchildren. You want for them all the things you can brag about. Everybody wants these things, but only the people who want them most will get them. The future is now. What will you teach your baby today? Who will they be tomorrow?

Looking out for number one is more than just good changing-table advice. From day one, you've got to instill a winning attitude in your infant. After all, nice babies finish last. So, push your kids! Teach them how to maneuver office politics, dress them for success, make them remember the full name of everyone they meet (to better win friends and influence people). Instruct them on how to manipulate social situations to get what they want, how to avoid dorky kids, and how to properly fold a business letter. Let them eat the olives from your martinis, give them every possible privilege, and of course, teach them not to take no for an answer.

You'll get just the kids you deserve.

What Did You Expect?

Now you're on your own.

You've read *What to Expect When Your Wife Is Expanding*, you've studied the advice and information, you've even looked up the hard words. You have devoted time and energy to preparing yourself for the dawn of fatherhood. Well done. Without intelligent, devoted readers like you, a moneymaking sequel would be impossible.

We have made every effort to be absolutely complete in our coverage of the issues and possibilities of pregnancy. We feel certain that answers to all your questions lie in these pages. Although we just realized that we forgot to write up that piece on taking a nonstress test—don't worry, there's nothing to it, really. Oh shoot, we didn't say anything about pre-pregnancy genetic counseling or choosing a godparent, either. We suppose it's a little late now. And we fully intended to provide a thorough discussion of the pros and cons of cesarean births from the father's perspective, but you can figure it out for yourself. We did mention Montgomery's tubercles, didn't we? Pretty sure we did. And bonding? We didn't do bonding, either? Well, it's important, so do it, and that's all you really need to know. Listen, maybe it wouldn't be such a bad idea to get ahold of some *other* guidebook to pregnancy, just sort of as a way to double-check. Oh shoot, we definitely should have done that feature on emergency delivery should you not get to the hospital on time.

Dad-to-be, just remember this: You can be pregnant and funny, but a hysterical pregnancy is no pregnancy at all. We're not sure what that means. But if you just remember it, maybe it'll keep you from worrying about other things too much.

Have a great pregnancy, a wonderful outcome—oh, and give our best regards to your wife.

Recommended Reading

Arms, Suzanne. *Immaculate Deception*. Boston: Houghton-Mifflin, 1975.

Brazelton, T. Berry. *Infants & Mothers*. New York: Delacorte, 1969.

Cannon, Hall, ed. *Cowboy Poetry: A Gathering*. Layton, Utah: Gibbs M. Smith, 1985.

Cerf, Bennett. *Riddle-De-Dee*. New York: Ballantine, 1962.

Dick-Read, Grantley. *Childbirth Without Fear*. New York: Harper & Row, 1972.

Eiger, M., and S. W. Olds. *The Complete Book of Breastfeeding*. New York: Bantam, 1973.

Eisenberg, Arlene, Heidi Eisenberg Murkoff, and Sandee Eisenberg Hathaway, R.N. *What to Expect When You're Expecting*, 3rd ed. New York: Workman Publishing, 2002.

Hill, Thomas. *TV Land to Go: The Big Book of TV Lists, TV Lore and TV Bests*. New York: Simon & Schuster, 2001.

___. *What the Heck Were You Expecting? A Complete Guide for the Perplexed Father*. New York: Three Rivers Press, 2000.

Kitzinger, Sheila. *The Complete Book of Pregnancy & Childbirth*. New York: Alfred A. Knopf, 1986.

Kunhardt, Dorothy. *Pat the Bunny*. New York: Western Publishing, 1991.

Leach, P. *Your Baby & Child*. New York: Alfred A. Knopf, 1978.

Leboyer, Frederick. *Birth Without Violence*. New York: Alfred A. Knopf, 1975.

Lewis, Michael. *Moneyball: The Art of Winning an Unfair Game*. New York: W. W. Norton, 2003.

Perec, Georges, and Gilbert Adair. *A Void.* (Translated from the French, *La Disparation*) New York: HarperCollins, 1995.

Steig, Irwin. *Poker for Fun & Profit*. New York: Astor-Honor, 1959.

Walker, Brian, ed. *The Best of Ernie Bushmiller's Nancy*. New York: Henry Holt & Company, 1988.

Weddle, Ethel H. *Walter Chrysler: Boy Machinist*. Childhood of Famous Americans Series. Indianapolis: Bobbs-Merrill, 1960.